T0132171

INSIGHT IS
20/20

Insights From a Higher Perspective for
Understanding the Purpose of Life

K.C. KYMBALL

BALBOA.
PRESS

A DIVISION OF HAY HOUSE

Balboa Press books may be ordered through booksellers or by contacting:

Balboa Press
A Division of Hay House
1663 Liberty Drive
Bloomington, IN 47403
www.balboapress.com
1 (877) 407-4847

Because of the dynamic nature of the Internet, any web addresses or links contained in this book may have changed since publication and may no longer be valid. The views expressed in this work are solely those of the author and do not necessarily reflect the views of the publisher, and the publisher hereby disclaims any responsibility for them.

The author of this book does not dispense medical advice or prescribe the use of any technique as a form of treatment for physical, emotional, or medical problems without the advice of a physician, either directly or indirectly. The intent of the author is only to offer information of a general nature to help you in your quest for emotional and spiritual well-being. In the event you use any of the information in this book for yourself, which is your constitutional right, the author and the publisher assume no responsibility for your actions.

Any people depicted in stock imagery provided by Getty Images are models, and such images are being used for illustrative purposes only.
Certain stock imagery © Getty Images.

Print information available on the last page.

ISBN: 978-1-5043-9612-7 (sc)
ISBN: 978-1-5043-9614-1 (hc)
ISBN: 978-1-5043-9613-4 (e)

Library of Congress Control Number: 2018900886

Balboa Press rev. date: 04/12/2018

For my sister Dawn Suzanne

"Within you is our eternal home. Open your heart and there you shall find us, basking in the glory of you."

The Apostles

CONTENTS

CHAPTER FOUR
Illuminating the Bible's Messages

CHAPTER FIVE
Science and Modern Medicine: Pathways to Truth

CHAPTER SIX
Creating Prosperity

CHAPTER SEVEN
Views from a Higher Perspective

CHAPTER EIGHT
Final Thoughts on the Power of Thought

"You have just stepped into the world of Spirit, which is your true home. Do not be afraid; simply sit back, relax and enjoy the ride. Nowhere on earth will you find an experience as exhilarating, mind-boggling and sensory stimulating as that you are about to encounter. May you find the answers you seek within your own heart, and may the words in this book serve to jump-start the memory of who you are."

The Apostles

"Life is but a dream, and wherever it takes you, you can be sure that you will awaken one day with a renewed sense of who you truly are."

"Time is of the essence means nothing to eternity."

"The mortality of humankind is but the ultimate contrast to the truth of immortality."

The Apostles

ACKNOWLEDGEMENTS

In loving memory of Leonard Belzer and Emily Squires.

To all my friends and family members who encouraged this book into existence, notably Sheri Lynn Evans, Kathie Ossing, Goldie Amira, Stacey Shumway-Johnson, Michelle Pritt-Boswell, Kevecca White, Pat Pritt, Emily Riley, Lori Martineau, Jim Lepley, and countless others. Thank you for your unwavering support.

My mother, Donna, who has been my constant companion throughout the process of awakening to other realities. She is proof positive that there are indeed angels among us.

Patricia Mischell, who completely changed my life.

My brothers, Daren and Dustin, who have shared the heartache of having lost a beloved sibling, along with the numerous lessons and gifts which have been gleaned from our experiences.

My son, Christopher, who has become not only a business partner, but also a wise friend and mentor on my never-ending journey toward spiritual enlightenment.

FOREWORD

Rarely do I find a book which I am unwilling to put down, and even *more* rarely do I find a book which I do not want to end. *Insight Is 20/20* is such a book. The wisdom and truth that unfolds within these pages as K.C Kymball shares with us what is being revealed to her through beings called "The Apostles" is overwhelming. It is a story about why we are here and reminds us that our lives *do* have a purpose, that there *is* a rationale behind all the beauty and magnificence of our world.

This book also tells us that, as we look back on the events of September 11, 2001, we may be able to understand the question we all have asked ourselves: Why? How could such evil happen? *Insight Is 20/20* explains why such events occur, and why we experience chaos, strife, pain and death in our world.

It is the story of our journey to meet life head on. K.C. shares with you information about God and higher states of consciousness, and how grief can be transformed into enlightenment. Above all, *Insight Is 20/20* defines our True Nature. It explains that death is not a taker of life, but rather a sustainer.

The author came to me at a time in her life when she was grieving for her sister who had recently passed away from a tragic death. It was through our conversations that I knew without a doubt that God would be touching K.C. in a very special way, and He has. These beautiful writings will touch your very soul. *Insight Is 20/20* is the result of her dedication to a greater understanding of the universe and our purpose for being here.

Unlike so many spiritual books on the market, this one-of-a-kind book has many unexpected twists that make it unique. Very rarely does a book cover the topic of death as eloquently as it is covered here. It is beautifully written and is astonishingly difficult to put down.

Most importantly, K.C. has written an indispensable book that is uplifting, empowering and comforting. Whether you're simply curious to learn more about your true nature, grieving the loss of a loved one, or frightened by what may come when it's your time to die, read on and experience for yourself the majesty of life.

My only complaint about this book is it's length; I kept wishing it were twice as long. During my whole life, if I could read only one book, this would be it. It's a must for everyone's library!

Patricia Mischell
patriciam.com
April, 2002

PREFACE

"If only you would lighten your load by removing negative thoughts, you too would fly like an angel."

The Apostles

Have you ever wondered why you're here? Does your life have a sense of purpose? Is there a rationale behind all the beauty and magnificence of our world, as well as behind the chaos and strife? What does it all mean? Where are we headed and from where have we come?

I have spent my life pondering these questions, but my attempts to gain clarity have often been frustrated by a society which deems all things as random and life itself to be pure chance. We are told that physical reality is that which can only be perceived by our five physical senses, but how reliable are our senses? After all, they tell us the Earth is stationary when we know that it's catapulting through outer space at a dizzying speed. Our physical senses also lead us to believe that the sun actually rises and sets each day, or that atoms and molecules don't exist. Animals are able to perceive many sounds and smells which remain elusive to us, but does that mean those things aren't real?

Life is all about perspectives, and we each have one—a different one. However, the thing we most need to realize is that we are not separate from one another. Rather, we are portions of one whole, viewing life from our unique vantage points. The Bible implies that there is only one son, and many people have taken this to mean that Jesus is the only son. If that's the case, where does that leave the rest of us? In reality, we are, collectively, that one son, seemingly separated fragments of one consciousness viewing life simultaneously from various perspectives, which is the meaning of omnipresence.

We are much more than we perceive ourselves to be. Believing that we are no more than our physical bodies is analogous to believing that a light bulb is the source of light. Our lives are meant to be an act of co-creatorship between our physical selves and that greater part of ourselves, the energy essence which animates our being. However, we disallow the entirety of that energy stream with the delusional belief that we are separate from it. Who we perceive ourselves to be is simply a portion of a much greater whole, but while we deny the greater part of ourselves access to us through our physical self, we are in a sense left to go it alone, which usually results in unnecessary pain and misery brought on by our "presumed" alienation. The truth is that we are never separated from the Whole. We only think we are. No one denies us anything—but we deny ourselves when we refuse to see the totality of our being.

The tragic death of my sister was the catalyst that enabled me to open to that greater aspect of myself which, by the way, is available to each of us—it's simply a matter of tuning in to it. There is no source of darkness, only a disallowance of the light of knowledge that brings with it greater awareness. With this awareness comes the peace, love, and harmony of our True-Selves, our highest potential. The desire to allow the light of truth into my life erupted from my experience with the pain and darkness associated with grief, for in our world—one of polarity, of contrast, we experience presumed darkness so we may better recognize and appreciate the light of who we really are.

The answers to what our real nature is are right under our noses. The term "enlightenment" means becoming aware of that which has always been present in the first place. A parable tells of a student fish asking the teacher fish, "What is this ocean I keep hearing about?" This precisely describes our situation. We are so surrounded by clues that we take them for granted, not even stopping to notice or appreciate the abundance of truth all around us. The truth has never been hidden from us; rather, we have chosen to ignore it, which is the true meaning of ignorance (ignorance). As humanity collectively rises above the illusory belief in negativity, we will begin to recognize the light of truth as it continually whispers its intimations to us in the form of flowers in the spring, birds in the sky, and berries on the vine. The vastness of the oceans, the countless grains of sand, the endless blue sky are there not only to behold, but to stand as symbols which serve to remind us of the absolute beauty and perfection, the vastness and endlessness of our true nature.

There is nothing we cannot be, do, or have. There are no limits to what we can experience other than the false beliefs in limitation we impose upon ourselves. By recognizing and accepting our Divinity, we sprout wings and soar free as a sparrow, to spread the light and love that we are to all corners of the planet.

For some time, humanity has erroneously been searching for answers outside of self, and it's time we own up to the fact that "our" way hasn't worked by allowing the greater all-knowing part of ourselves the opportunity to hold the reins. By so doing, we are in no way surrendering our free will. Rather, we are integrating our conscious, physical self with our Divine self, which empowers us with the strength of the entire universe. We give up nothing, but we gain everything by allowing ourselves to recognize our full potential.

I first met "The Apostles" while attempting to write about my experiences with grief after the death of my sister. I spent lots of time compiling questions, but as I sat down to answer them, I kept running into dead ends.

Then I attended a seminar held by Patricia Mischell regarding life after death, where I was introduced to the subject of channeling. At first it seemed silly to me, but, nonetheless, I decided to give it a try.

So I sat down with my pile of questions before me, and asked for help. Immediately, I got a response. Words seemed to flow out of nowhere, but because they felt so much like my own thoughts, I struggled for a while with the validity of the entire experience. However, after months of presenting various questions and consistently receiving eloquent answers, I began to trust that I was not alone in this game called life. Call it Higher Self, Spiritual Guides, Universal Mind. All I know is that on my own, I am not capable of producing such grandiose information.

When I asked for their names, they assured me that from where they hailed, names were unnecessary. But to appease me I was told I could refer to them as "The Apostles." I hurriedly looked up the word "Apostle" in the dictionary and found the words: "One who initiates or first advocates a great reform; messenger; spreader of the faith or truth; divine representative or spokesman." How fitting.

The guidance I continue to receive from "The Apostles" has helped me and those closest to me tremendously in our search for the meaning of life. Their wisdom amazes and delights me, and I can only hope that my translations do justice to the unconditional love and admiration I feel as I'm receiving this information. May you, too, begin to recognize your own inherent power, to receive this universal Wisdom, so that together we can create a harmonious world. Keep in mind as you're reading these words that *you* are the kingdom, *you* are the way, and *you* are the truth and the light. The sooner we accept these facts individually, the sooner we will collectively illuminate our darkened paths. One of our greatest teachers said, "The kingdom of heaven is within you." He also said, "Seek ye first the kingdom," and that should be easy, now that we know where to look.

From this point on "The Apostles" speak succinctly for themselves.

CHAPTER ONE

The Nature of Earthly Reality

"You are not merely a human being having an Earth-life experience; you are the creator of the human being having an Earth-life experience."

"The greatest purpose the ego serves is that it allows one the opportunity to rise above it."

The Apostles

Did God Create the Earth? If Not,
How Was It Created and Why?

Before answering this question, we must remind you of the truth of Oneness. All things in this vast and glorious universe are of the one Mind of God. Nothing exists outside of mind, and therefore nothing is separate from the Universal Mind. Each of you exists as a spark of consciousness, a thought within the one great Mind, and you cannot separate a thought from its thinker. Thus, we can conclude that the thinker and the thought are one, and in reality, there is only one thinker and therefore only one thought. This one thought has divided and subdivided, portraying different aspects of itself through various realities, such as that of Earth. Now you, as the thought, are forever connected to the thinker, which many refer to as God. You can never be separate from God, for *you* are God; you are His creation, His thought, and you exist for eternity as a thought within His Mind, which encompasses the entire universe.

Why are we explaining all this to you? To answer the question to the best of our abilities, we felt it necessary to remind you of the true nature of All-That-Is. By so doing, we hope to create a clearer picture which will enable you to see yourself in your true state, which is as a thought within the Mind of God. So when you ask who created the Earth, you will be able to understand our answer, which is: God created the Earth, for God is all there is, you see. Many of you may be asking why a loving God would have created such a place, fraught with madness and negativity.

We say to you that it was merely an aspect of God-consciousness (which constitutes each of you in earthly form) which brought the Earth plane, devoid of all light, into being. Let us return to the separation (by "separation" we mean that spark of consciousness which became a dream of separation within the one Mind of God). All the peoples of the Earth exist as aspects of that single thought or dream, hence your oneness or connectedness with each other. You have merely become seemingly separated fragments of this one thought of separation, and you are thereby carrying out roles that you've given yourselves in order to prove the insanity of such a notion. God, the Infinite Mind, is forever expanding by producing more thought. And once the thought of a physical reality––one in which the illusion of separation played a role––was formed, then off you went as the thought itself to explore this concept more fully, expanding upon this single thought by your interaction within it. So here you are, dear ones, acting within the dream of physicality in order to take thought to a point it has never gone to before.

Utilizing your creative powers as aspects of God, co-creators with the Universal Mind, you have brought the Earth plane into existence through your willingness to participate within it. Who then created the Earth plane, you or God? Both are correct, for remember that you cannot separate yourself from God, just as you cannot separate the thinker from the thought, or the perceiver from the perceived. You are one entity, one Mind, divided into seemingly separate aspects of itself. You would not exist without the one great Mind which brought you into existence. So, as you sit and contemplate all this, realize that in reality you have never been separate from your Father, who conceived you as a thought; you have merely spun a web of illusion for yourself which says to you that you exist outside the Father's Mind, or separately from God. Again, this has never been the case, but through your willingness to believe as such, you are creating new worlds, new heavens, which serve to expand the universe's knowledge of itself. We must point out, however, that God exists as a state of bliss, of pure love and knowledge, which has always been and will always be. With each interaction as physical beings upon your physical plane, you are merely seeking to reunite your current "self" with this highest state of all-knowing, and you accomplish this by exploring the far reaches of Mind, such as that of physicality.

Thus, God has always been and always will be a state of pure bliss that patiently awaits your return, for never has this state ceased to *be*. Furthermore, this state exists within each of you as a potential waiting to be "tapped." Once you've tapped this potential within yourself, you shall return home to the loving arms of God with the full realization that the God-state of knowing is where you belong. Many have asked if God is aware of the turmoil and darkness we are experiencing on Earth. Our answer is unequivocally no, for remember, God exists as the highest state of pure bliss and can therefore know nothing but the peace, love, and harmony of Itself. You are merely aspects of God who have wandered off into presumed darkness, a state of "forgetting." Until you are ready to rejoin the rest of yourself in the state of eternal bliss, God shall wait patiently as the highest state of being and shall welcome your arrival with open arms. You are loved and cherished as the children, the thought of God, and once you have fully realized this fundamental truth, you shall find yourself amidst the state of pure bliss, knowing full well your right to be there.

Commend yourself for your efforts to bring the light of knowledge to the Earth plane, but know too that God would prefer to have His children dwell within His mansions of truth, rather than within the straw huts you've built for yourselves through the illusion of unworthiness. Come home, children, where you belong, and know that only peace, love, and harmony await you. God has not gone anywhere, and neither have you, for that matter; you only think you have. Awaken now and realize who you truly are and the universe shall be eternally grateful, for God shall then have all His children home.

How Do You View Humankind and Our Lives Here On Earth?

Have you ever watched children at play, perhaps as they pretend to be little warriors carrying around imaginary guns and slinging imaginary arrows back and forth, as if they were capable of harming one another? As you watch the little ones, you are oftentimes amused by the extent of their illusion and how very real their imaginary play world can seem to them. Yet you are not caught up in their dramas, for you are viewing life from a different perspective and therefore you have a stronger grasp upon what you call reality.

Although the games children play are very real to them, they do not affect you, for you know that in reality their imaginary world does not exist. So, you allow them to play along, creating up a storm, as you go about your life from your higher perspective. Oftentimes you think this form of playacting is cute, and you know that at the very least it's serving to enhance their state of creativity, thus adding unto their knowledge of life. The way in which we view humankind, from our higher perspective, is not much different from that, you see. As we view your dramas and all your earthly woes, we see it not from the perspective of the child who's caught up in the drama and believes in that drama, but rather from a state of awareness which allows us greater insight into knowing that all is well upon your planet, whether you perceive it to be so or not. We know you are merely creating dramas in which to participate in order to learn a thing or two about life in general. Know that all is One. From where we sit, we know that we are not separate from one another; you are an aspect of who we are, and vice versa. Therefore, there is no difference in who we are––merely a difference in what we are experiencing at this particular time. We are not better than you, nor are we more knowing. We simply have better seats, so to speak, in this particular play, which allow us to view each act from a better angle, that is all. As you go about creating your life dramas for yourself, realize that all is as it should be and don't get so caught up in the snares of Earth-life illusion. Lighten up and enjoy yourself, dear ones, and you shall begin to view your own life from a higher perspective––the better seats which we now occupy.

It seems as if all sorts of symbols surround us here on Earth that serve to remind us of our true state of being. Could you describe some of the most prevalent ones, along with their meanings?

When you journeyed to Earth school, you did so with one thought in mind: to know your self more fully. By this, we mean that in order for you to become more perfect creators of only love and harmony, it is necessary for you to fully understand the nature of who you are. You are each grand and glorious energy beings, majestic creators, and the Earth plane offers the perfect opportunity for you to realize your potential. Through your creative abilities, you fashioned this Earth plane for yourself, to be used as a school of sorts in which you could test your abilities and learn more about the Truth. Earth school can then be likened to a testing ground which offers many opportunities for growth through spiritual awareness. We must point out, however, that your time here was not meant to be lived in fear. Rather, your sole (soul) intention in creating the Earth plane was to offer yourself a joyous learning experience. Therefore, we would urge you to rise above the ego state of self-centered consciousness so that you may glean all you can from your Earth-life experience in a more joyful manner.

Of course, when you created the Earth plane you were fully aware of the intent behind this action. You therefore purposely created it with many "props" or clues which would serve to remind you of who you truly are. Here we will offer you a few of these reminders in the hope that our words will stimulate you to further searching, thereby adding unto your joyful life experiences.

The first and most prevalent source of reminders which serve you in your earthly state are the stars. They exist as glorious, radiating temples of light capable of being seen with the physical eye. The magic induced within your being by the twinkling of the stars oftentimes stirs feelings of awe and inspiration as you dwell upon the vastness of the universe. You created the stars, as well as the moon, to remind yourself of your own awe-inspiring capabilities as you traverse throughout your day-to-day lives. You, dear ones, are the creators of this vast universe and all the stars existing within its spheres. The next time you gaze upon the stars in your nightly sky, allow the truth of your being to spring forth from your heart, enabling you to hear the whisperings of the universe as it speaks to you through each emanating beam of light, beckoning you Home. Know that the stars you see exist not outside yourself, as your physical perceptions would have you believe——rather, they are *within* you, within your perceptions. Each time you look upon the sky, you are re-creating the stars through the power of your thoughts. You cannot separate the perceiver from the perceived. Therefore, you cannot separate yourself from the stars.

It is a powerful thought, is it not?

The sun also serves as a powerful reminder of your beginnings. It is the star with which many of you are most familiar, for it serves to light your days and nourish your entire planet. You have centered your days, weeks, months, and years around this magnificent star. Without the brilliance of the sun, you would have no Earth school.

The light which emanates from the sun, giving life to all species upon your plane, is but a minute replica of the light of All-That-Is, of which you are a part. Just as the sun feeds and nourishes all life upon your planet, offering its radiance and love unconditionally, so too is this true of our one great Father, who shines more brightly than 10,000 suns, offering His love and light to all.

The purpose of your sun is also to remind you of the true working order of the universe. The Earth and the way it orbits your sun are fashioned by the same mechanics which propel the universe. You could say that each of you is a miniature Earth orbiting our one great Father, who can be likened to the sun. It is a potent reminder of the brilliance which exists within each of you. Just as you derive your physical life from the energy of the sun, so too do you derive the life force which powers your entire state of being from the energy source of All-That-Is.

There are numerous examples—as a matter of fact, nothing within your current Earth frame of mind doesn't serve this purpose of "reminding," but we will only touch upon a few reminders here, for it is not possible to list them all.

Flowers are a wonderful example of the beauty that lies within you. Flowers represent your inner beauty and also serve to remind you of your elegant powers of creativity. Notice the vast array of flowers upon your planet—their various hues, mixed and matched, spotted and striped, vibrant and alive—they are works of art. *Your* works of art. A great deal of love and thought were put into the creation of each and every flower, for they are the living reminders of the limitlessness to your creative abilities. The same holds true for the many animal species in your world, most notably the birds and fish, for many of these creatures offer the spectacular brilliance of your creative genius. In your world, there are birds of such vibrant color that it boggles the mind, and fish sporting such animated beauty that one oftentimes stares in amazement at them. Many of you even enjoy encasing these creatures within your homes to more readily reflect upon their beauty. Did you think, dear ones, that all this happened by chance? No, each and every creature upon your planet was created by you, and for you to enjoy and behold. Even the word "creature" is derived from the word "create." As you scurry about from one dilemma to the next, your artwork stands in the shadows, whispering the truth regarding the nature of your being.

The variations amongst your animal kingdom also serve the same purpose: The beautiful stripes on the tiger's back, as well as the spots on the leopard, are merely more of your creations, your artwork in physical form.

You are limitless in your powers to create, and even as we speak, you are adding unto the creating of the universe with the thoughts you think each and every moment. This is what is meant when we say that the universe is an ever-expanding creative universe, for there is no end or limit to creation. The universe is forever in a state of "becoming," and you, dear creators, are the impetus behind this growth. You are the creators, co-creators with God, of all that is and all that ever shall be. Awaken now and begin to realize the powers you wield in order to accept yourself as Divine aspects of the Whole, thereby claiming your thrones in Heaven.

We would like to point out that many of the words you use to describe a particular thing are proof of your greater knowing. For instance, the very word "planet" is derived from your inner knowing, which says to you that there are in reality no "places," but rather "planes" of thought or existence. With your word "planet," you have merely taken this knowledge and added a "T" to the end. Plane-t. Coincidence? There is no such thing.

As we speak of planes of existence, there is another word which is commonly used to describe this same notion, and that being the word "state." From your all-knowing, higher perspective, you were aware of this fact when you began to form the country in which many of you now live——America, the United *States* of. Whether you reside in the state of California or the state of Ohio, or the state of confusion, it does not matter, for your state of mind is all there is. In actuality, you do not move from place to place, merely from state to state. Your naming of this is correct. However, your perceptions of it are not.

Another good example where the use of words is necessitated is the word "evil." The very word is simply the reversal of the word "live." You see, evil stems only from one's inability to see his Divine potential within himself. It is a form of non-living. In other words, when one is said to be evil, he is merely not living within the desired state of being. Evil, then, is simply the opposite of "live", for when one forgets his true nature, he often becomes frustrated in his attempts to find the goodness (Godness) within himself, thus acting out in a way not conducive to that of Truth. And the word "devil" is merely a metaphor which stems from this same truth: It is the word "evil" with a "d" placed before it.

You see, dear ones, your world is full of reminders and examples of your inner knowing. The next time you eat fruit from a tree or pick berries from a vine, or prepare dinner with your potatoes, lettuce, and tomatoes from the garden, realize that these are all things which you have designed to fulfill your needs as you are interacting as humans upon this physical plane. Everything you need is readily available to you from the earth itself. You, as glorious, magnificent creators, would have it no other way. Therefore, as you go about your daily life, oftentimes living amidst utter chaos and confusion, stop to smell the roses or taste the sweetness of the fruits, or marvel at the beauty of the birds in your sky and know full well that there really is order to the wondrousness of life. What are the odds, dear ones, that it could be any other way?

How do our present personalities differ from our True-Selves?

Your True-Self or Higher-Self differs from your present personality in that it is a much broader, expanded aspect of the Whole than that which you consciously perceive as self. By this, we mean that who you are now is only a minute portion of your True-Self. Many refer to the True-Self as Higher-Self or Soul (among other variations) and that is okay, for names do not matter, nor do they alter the truth one iota. You, your present personality, can be likened to an ocean wave, and we will say that the wave is who you are currently experiencing yourself to be, while the ocean is your True-Self. And although you may oftentimes feel separated from this source, or True-Self, you are, in actuality, no more separate than a wave is from the ocean. You see, when you decided to don physicality, you did so merely through your intentions, your thoughts, which govern all you do. As you set forth your intentions to form a personality which would become "you" in this lifetime, so it was. But only a minute portion or aspect of your True-self has come forth into this physical expression of life. Your true state of being knows this, but many of you are not consciously aware of the truths of which we speak, for in your "forgetting," you oftentimes learn your greatest lessons. If you were to remember all that which you already know, you would not be so compelled to go forth within this physical existence to seek more knowledge to add unto All-That-Is.

Everything you say, do, or experience adds unto the knowledge of the universe. There are no mistakes, dear ones, merely added knowledge. Your present personality is only a creation gathered from the huge store of data that makes up your Higher-Self.

In other words, when you fashioned your current personality, you merely took from your higher Source a sprinkling of this knowing and a dusting of that knowing, which comes from the pool of all the lifetimes and experiences you've ever had, you see. You created your personality according to the agenda you had set forth for yourself during your current incarnation. It is much like creating from a recipe; you take some of this and some of that, and then you mix it all together to form a creation, which in this instance is that of a personality. Thus, who you are now is a very small portion of who you truly are, and who you truly are knows all there is to know about anything and everything. Although it may seem as if you do not have access to this vast store of knowledge, we can assure you that all the knowledge of the universe is available to you simply for the asking. But to tap into this source of knowledge, you must learn to rise above the ego state of consciousness. Then you shall be given all the answers you seek. And this, dear souls, is all part of the learning process which takes place amidst the Earth state of being.

Where do you suppose all the so-called geniuses in your society got their knowledge? How do you think the man known as Einstein was able to do all that which gave him the label of genius? Einstein, we might add, was willing to share information regarding his access to knowledge, but the peoples were not ready to hear him. Your True-Self is an all-knowing, projected aspect of All-That-Is, and your present personality is merely a minute portion of your True-Self. In other words, you are an aspect of an aspect of God. And so it goes.... There is nothing else, you see. Know that as you tool around in your day-to-day lives, you are constantly adding unto the vast store of knowledge that constitutes your Higher-Self and All-That-Is, or God. All that which you think, do and experience in this lifetime greatly assists in the evolve-ment of All. Your work here is of great importance, and in order to fully assist in the growth of All-That-Is, you need to see yourself as much more than only your present personality, for you *are* much more than you perceive yourself to be. Begin giving credit where credit is due and you shall find yourself quickly amidst the higher realms of consciousness with the full realization of who you truly are, and your work here shall be all the more gratifying.

Why are there different races and languages on Earth?

Before answering this question, we must first remind you of the reasoning behind your humanness. Firstly, from the Soul perspective there are many advantages to being human. The most basic one is that it allows you ample opportunity to discover the truth of your nature. Couple that with the diverse aspects of being human and you shall quickly come to the conclusion that by offering different races, you are offered a smorgasbord of opportunities from which to learn; thus, you are never at a loss for growth. The different races were created from the need to provide a variety of circumstances which would serve to enhance the advancement of the Whole. In reality, you are never separate from your brothers, no matter what the color of your skins. You are each aspects of the One Mind, divided into seemingly separate portions.

This recognition is quite possibly the biggest hurdle you must clear on your earthly path toward enlightenment. Many prejudices have sprung from the deep-seated fear of one's outer appearance being different from that of your own. We would urge you, peoples of the Earth, to seek to understand one another's cultures so that you may find love where now there appears to be only strife. This is an important factor in regard to Earth's current road to enlightenment, and most notably in the United States of America, where much segregation has come about due to the lack of communication with, and knowledge of the various ethnic backgrounds. Due to this lack of knowledge, other cultures will eventually find in your country a perfect example of what not to do. This is how it should be, for you live in a world of great contrast, and the best way to learn about unconditional love is by experiencing the lack of it, which, by the way, can only be illusory.

Do not think that we are attempting to instill fear in those of you who call yourselves Americans. Rather, our intent is to remind you of your true purpose for being here as humans, and to let you know that although times may seem hard and the road seems rocky, this is not in actuality the case. You need only open your heart to know that all is well. The day will come upon your planet when you will see others for what they truly are––extensions of yourself. This path will be chosen one way or another, but it is up to you to choose the easy path, simply by choosing love.

The numerous languages of your world have also caused much segregation, but this too serves a purpose. We know this is difficult for many of you to see amidst the turmoil which currently abounds, but, nonetheless, it is so. All things serve a grand purpose, which is always for the "better-ment" of the Whole. Begin looking to one another for support and encouragement, rather than facing off in battles of contempt. Realize that racial or language differences need not create barriers between the brothers of Earth––in reality, they do quite the opposite.

Your differences will eventually bring you together in a way which will cause the emergence of greater comprehension about who you truly are. Learn to replace fear with love where those who are unlike yourself are concerned. This is the true plan and the reasoning behind all your current dilemmas, for it is in the removal of fear as a reality that love can move in and take its place. Look to your neighbors, no matter what their races, and begin to see yourself. Only then will Earth be headed "due Home." Release yourself now from the bondage of hatred––which does not exist in reality––and begin to accept one another fully. The different races offer you the perfect opportunity to see the various aspects of yourself in all your glory, and in a different light. Realize that each race and language blossomed from your very own creativity. You, dear souls, have created the entire world upon which you walk in order to expand your appreciation of yourself. Therefore, it is fitting to say that each race of human being––as well as all other lifeforms––is merely a work of art––your art. Learn to love and cherish your artwork as a mother cherishes a child. Simply put, you are the sole (Soul) creator of yourself and each other, and only when you allow your heart to lead will you begin to act like who you truly are. Realize this fact, children of the Earth, and bring yourself and your planet Home by releasing the seeds of love which exist within your very being.

Help us understand the time/space illusion. How can we see relics from our past if there is no past? How can all things be happening simultaneously and in the present? Does this mean that the soldiers in World War I continue to battle somewhere in eternity?

We know the difficulty those of you in human form have comprehending our messages; however, we ask that you try to understand them. Whether you know it or not, dear ones, you hold all the knowledge of the universe within your being, and you need only learn to dodge the ego in order to reach that vast store of information.

Our main purpose is to remind you that you are *not* your bodies, nor are you your egos. Your True-Self has never left Home; only an aspect of yourself has ventured forth into an illusory state of being, which has made you feel as if you are separate and alone. Never has this been the case, but due to the delusional state of mind in which you have become so enmeshed, you are often unable to decipher the Truth. Therein lie the reasons behind the current dilemma, which restricts you from seeing beyond linear time/ space constraints. You are not, however, a hopeless case. Rather, the opposite is true. You are God's children, inheritors of the universe, and worthy of all the riches of His kingdom. It is your birthright, dear ones. We would urge you to begin reclaiming the crowns and jewels you have previously shunned. In order to fully understand the nature of the universe––which does not include time and space––you must relinquish the ego's present stranglehold upon your senses.

Only then can comprehension be realized. We hope to help you rise above the ego with our words. We shall attempt to paint a picture of Truth which will activate your intuitive powers. When we speak of Truth, it is always in regard to the truth of Oneness. The ego has placed many constraints upon the peoples of Earth which have served to create a mockery of Oneness. For instance, the ego says to you that all things are bound by time/space constraints, and that all things are separate from yourself. This is simply not so. Begin now, children, to reverse this way of thinking. Literally turn it completely around and see the opposite side of the coin, for the opposite side of ego-generated "non-sense" is always that of Truth. The ego knows of no other way to create falsehoods than to flip the coin over, so to speak. Therefore, we can deduce that if all is indeed not separate from one's self, then all must be a part of oneself––within you, in fact.

You, dear ones, are not separate from anything, for you *are* the universe. If the ego tells you that time and space exist, thereby separating you from All-That-Is, this too is untrue. "How can time and space not exist when archaeologists are constantly finding relics from the past," you might ask. Again, as long as the ego is in its current place of "rule-ment", you cannot fully comprehend these truths. It is true that archaeological digs all over your planet are unearthing what appear to be relics from the ancient past, but this too is untrue. Remember, only the ego says to you that a thing is old and a thing is new. Let us go back to the time when you first made your earthly journeys. You knew that in order to believe in the illusion of time and space (which was concocted for a reason), you would need props to make the "play" convincing. You are no dummies, dear ones, and in order to move into the illusional Earth-frame of mind, it had to seem real.

Now, you may be asking, "Why would I have created such a state, complete with ego, in order to merely bind myself into some kind of mess?" We say that, as with all things, there is a grand purpose to this chaos and confusion, and you, dear souls, are the sole creators. You are wisdom personified, and you need only trust your Higher-Self. In the truest sense, you know exactly what you are doing. Therefore, yes, it is true that the relics you uncover from the bed of the earth are indeed real; at least real enough that you have been able to believe your very own illusion. See how brilliant you are? It surely takes pure genius in order to deceive oneself so well, don't you think? The ego, too, was created in order for humankind to see themselves as partially separated from the Whole, which would, in the long run, allow for more expansion and greater awareness of your true state of being. In other words, the ego offers the perfect contrast to Truth, which serves to stimulate you to further creativity. However, an "error" was made when the ego was allowed to override your connection to the God-Source in such a way that it seemed as if you were not a part of God at all. When speaking of "errors," we must remind you that in actuality, there are no errors. But we are speaking to those of you who believe in illusion and therefore must use the word within your linear vocabulary which best serves to get our point across. (It is important to remember this at all times when you are mulling over our words, for we are immensely limited by the restrictions of using a linear vocabulary, and with such limitations, we cannot possibly do justice to the Truth).

So the ego serves a grand purpose, but it must not be allowed to continue its current rampage, and only you, dear peoples of the Earth, can stop it. The ego is your creation, fashioned from your own thought forms, and due to free will, only you can make these changes. We only ask that you look to your heart for guidance, for we no longer wish to see our brothers and sisters on the Earth plane living amidst seeming pain and poverty. It need not be this way for you to learn from your Earth school.

Now, when you posed the question before us regarding World War I soldiers battling it out forever, we had to chuckle with amusement at this thought, for we oftentimes forget the extent of your dramatic Earth illusions. However, we do not wish to poke fun; we merely wish to make light of a situation in the hope that you too will see the light in all things of presumed darkness upon your planet.

Firstly, in reality, there was no war and there shall never be war, for how can you have war and hatred and violence of any kind when these things are merely delusional aspects of the ego mind? Do you see how this works? The only place evil exists is as a delusional thought form amidst the ego, which itself does not exist in reality. So, if you can see that the ego is an illusion, then you can also see that all creations of the ego, such as war, are illusions as well.

No, dear souls, armies are not battling it out forever in eternity, for in harmony, there is no violence. Ponder this: There is no death, so how can there be war? There is no violence, so how can there be bloodshed? There is no hatred, so how can there be conflicting opinions which create such heated non-sense? No, dear souls, you have truly allowed your egos to run wild with your senses, and it is time this stops so you can all return Home, bringing your planet with you. Know that in Truth there is only peace, love, light, and harmony.

The next time you open a history book which speaks to you of war, realize that history itself is an illusion, so too then is war. War exists only as a spark of illusion amidst the far reaches of the human ego-mind. Realize this and do not fear war, or anything for that matter, for we can also throw fear into the melting pot of illusion. Look to your past not as gospel, but rather as "props" serving a grand purpose. Learn from your "history," and you shall quickly stamp out illusion altogether. Know that your seeming past does exist eternally, but within a state of bliss and union amidst the vastness of the ever-evolving universe. And this, dear souls, is what it's all about. We live in an ever-evolving, creative universe that's only purpose is to expand itself by more fully understanding its true nature. You are this universe, and you are currently entangled in yet another web of illusion which you've spun for yourself via your creative powers in order to see yourself in a new and better light. This is Truth. You need look no farther to find yourself than that of your neighbors and the grass and the trees. These things *are* you, dear ones, wrapped up neatly in a package labeled Earth. Once this is fully realized, you will have completed your treacherous journeys, and you shall have come to know yourself as the God-Source of All-That-Is.

What is the "Divine Plan" we've heard so much about?

The Divine Plan you refer to is but the perpetuation of Truth upon your Earth plane. You see, when you first journeyed into physicality, you did so with the intention of ridding yourself of any and all notions of negativity and separation. Negativity, as you know it, does not exist in reality, but somewhere along the way you've become split from the One Source, from God, in your thinking. In other words, you deviated from the Source in such a way that you have deemed yourself separate from it. Once the thought of seeming separation, or splitting, occurred, the universe was obligated to allow you to see it through.

You are grand creators, and each thought you think brings forth some form of manifestation, be it physical or non-physical, according to the nature of the thought. Once the notion of separation was conceived, it began to expand itself into the far reaches of Mind until it seemingly became so real (much like the snowball effect), that it had to be played out, so to speak, in order for you to come full circle, back to the Source which created you.

Again, never have you been separate from the Source, but your belief in that apparent separation is what brought the Earth plane into existence. We often refer to it as "Earth school," for as you are interacting upon this physical plane, acting out the dramas within the play of earth-life, much learning is derived. We refer to it as "coming full circle." If you picture a circle, you will see that it is one continuous line which begins and ends at the same point. We refer to this to remind you that you have not actually gone anywhere; you simply believe that you have and are just in the process of realizing this fact, finding your way back to the point that you never really left in the first place. That, dear souls, is the Divine Plan.

The Divine Plan begins with Truth and ends with Truth. When you journeyed to the Earth, you began with Truth and turned it upside down to create the Earth plane, which is the exact opposite of Truth. And as you wind your way along your paths, shedding light upon one falsehood after another, uncovering a portion of Truth with each insight, you are participating in the process of evolution. Once that process has been completed, you shall return to the place, or rather, the state from which you originated, but with a much greater understanding of who you are. There is a purpose to all things which always serves to expand the universe's knowledge of Itself.

So you see, dear ones, you are magnificent creators who have fashioned the Earth plane in order to bring yourself more fully (meaning with more awareness), to your rightful state of God-consciousness. It all began with one thought––*I am separate from my Father*, and it shall end with one thought: *I and my Father are One.* The latter has always been the case, but you needed to find out for yourself, and what better way to achieve greater understanding of your true nature than by interacting upon a plane which offers the perfect contrast to Truth? By experiencing illusion and contrast, you enhance your appreciation of your highest state of being. In other words, what better way to recognize what you *do* want than by experiencing that which you *don't* want? By participating within the illusion, little by little you begin to spark the memory of who you truly are (evolution), and as you do so, you move closer and closer to Home.

Therefore, because you had the thought of separation, it had to be carried out in a way that would allow you to see the madness of such a notion for yourself. It is a wondrous plan, and it has served its purpose indeed, for many of you have come to know yourselves, thus enabling you to spread the love that you are throughout the universe. All is well and the plan is perfect. You created it and you interact within it to serve a grand purpose. Trust your Self, dear ones, to bring yourself and your planet Home, for only perfection can be squeezed from perfection, and absolute perfection is precisely who you are.

Knowing that a macrocosm is the whole universe, I've often heard humans being described as microcosms, which is a miniature world or universe. Is this a fair assumption?

It is important you begin to see yourself on a grander scale than that of a miniature replica. You *are* the universe, dear ones, not some smaller portion or representation thereof.

CHAPTER TWO

The Nature of the Universe

"The only reality is life: All else is but illusion."

"The belief in linear time is humanity's attempt to chop eternity into pieces."

The Apostles

Define Real Time.

Real time, in Truth, is no-time, because time, as you know it, does not exist. Linear time as it pertains to your Earthly experience is merely a creation of the dualistic ego mind which allows you to believe in separateness. In other words, time enhances the belief that you are separate or disconnected from Source. The belief in linear time also produces boundaries in which the drama of earth-life can unfold. All things existing within this vast and glorious universe were created within the One Mind of God, at the very same instant.

For instance, the Earth and all things of it, including all potential time frame realities, were created at the speed of a thought. As you interact with one another here in this current physical reality, you are merely expanding upon that one thought. All of this takes place simultaneously within the Mind of God, rather than in linear fashion, such as that which is represented by your belief in past and future. We understand the difficulty the ego has comprehending this truth, for that is the way ego was created. In other words, it's simply doing its job. In Truth, all things exist in the eternal "now," which simply means that all that ever was and all that ever shall be already exist within the one great Mind.

As you go forth to experience one reality or another, such as your current "now," you are merely flitting in and out of these various realities. You literally said, "Hmm, that looks interesting, let's go over there and see what we can experience," and off you went to explore and perhaps alter the beliefs of a certain era. As you can see, the "past" is not set in stone, nor is the future, for you each have the capacity to go in and out (through your projection of will), to each and every reality existing in the universe at any time you so desire. We might add, you are not limited to Earth realities, for there are many realities of which you are currently unaware. You experience these realities all the time, especially during your sleep state, which, again, you are unaware of. "But why are we unable to remember this in our waking state?" you might ask. It is for this reason: To remain fully focused upon a specific time/space reality (also known as probable or parallel reality), it was agreed that the memory of other realities had to be left behind. Otherwise, you would find yourself deluged with the enormity of your entire existence and be unable to focus upon only one reality at a time.

If you think you have problems letting go of the past now, imagine what would happen if you could remember all of your various "pasts." You would simply carry the memory of other realities around with you, much like excess baggage, which would render you incapable of fully focusing on your current reality. And this "forgetting" pertains only to your conscious ego selves. There is a broader, expanded, all-knowing part of yourself that is simultaneously aware of all the lifetimes you have ever lived. Many refer to this as "Soul," or Higher-Self. Remember, all is one, and who you perceive yourself to be in this lifetime is simply a small portion or aspect of the Whole. Thus, you are in actuality living amongst all the various realities simultaneously. You, your ego self, is just unaware of where the rest of yourself is focused.

As we've said, the various realities you call past and future are not fixed. Rather, they are variable. That's why they are oftentimes referred to as *probable* realities, because, in truth, nothing is reality, for all is forever in constant, forward-changing motion. What we refer to as probable reality is determined by the mass consciousness of those who are participating within it at any given time. This can change from moment to moment as those within a certain probable reality choose to alter their vibrations by raising their awareness to a point above (or below) that which was intended.

Each and every reality is constantly fluctuating, thus the term "probable," for we each have the ability to alter any reality at any time in any way we see fit. Thus we can conclude that the past is not set in stone, nor is the future predetermined. All realities exist within the Now as potentials, forever in the state of becoming perfected. By "perfected," we mean reaching the state in which only peace, love, and harmony abound, commonly referred to as God, or the Heaven state of consciousness.

Picture a large auditorium filled with numerous stages, and upon each stage, rehearsals are being held for various plays. Let us say that your role is to keep an eye on these plays, roving back and forth from one to the other, offering your insights from an outsider's point of view, which will perhaps serve to alter or change the course of these plays. As you offered your insight and knowing from your different perspective, those participating within the plays would possibly change a line here or there, or perhaps they would decide to add an entirely new ending to the drama. Whatever the case, it would be clear that those participating within the plays would have the free will to either take your advice or leave it. The way in which time works in reality is not much different from this. The words we offer you are merely from an outsider's perspective, for we are capable of viewing your Earth-life dramas from a different vantage point. We are here simply to offer our insight and knowing in order to perhaps enhance or alter the outcome of this particular play, but it is you––the actual participants within the play––who have the final say.

Therefore, picture the universe as a large and constantly expanding set of stages, each occupied by a particular play (which you've termed past and future). Now, see that these plays are occurring simultaneously upon the grand stage of life amidst the one mind of God. Then you will have a clearer picture of "real" time. You, as individual sparks of the One Mind, have unlimited access to each of these plays (or realities), which means that you can (and do) enter into these various plays at any time you desire, to explore within and/or expand upon that which has been offered thus far. Expansion and "evolve-ment" are the key words here, for the universe, the One Mind of God, is forever expanding and evolving within Itself. This is accomplished by your interactions, as aspects of God, within each of these probable realities. There is no stagnation in the universe––only growth. You, as energy beings, are continually recycling yourselves, in and out, in and out, of various realities to expand upon that which has already been thought, so that thought itself may be taken to a point it has never gone to before. This, dear souls, is the whole gist of your being, the very nature of the universe itself.

Imagine the universe as an enormous playground filled with all sorts of delights and experiences which are yours for the taking. There is some of everything that has ever been thought of in this vast universe (just as there is on Earth, but on a much smaller scale). Enjoy your time here, dear ones, for this is precisely where you've chosen to be focused. You have always had, and you will always continue to have an eternity in which to explore and savor all the richness life has to offer. Lighten up and no longer allow time to be your enemy. Realize that time, in Truth, is a "no-thing"; it simply does not exist. Eternity is all there is and *now* is the only reality.

Recognize that as you participate within this current lifetime, you are simultaneously participating within *all* lifetimes, for there is neither end nor beginning to creation––there is only the steady, rhythmic flowing of ceaseless eternity, of which you are forever a part. Rejoice in this knowledge and allow your True-Self to outshine the ego's system of time/space illusion. You shall then find yourself fully conscious and awake, able to savor every moment of this delectable Earth-life experience.

What are some of the laws which govern the universe?

The laws which govern the universe are not laws in the same sense as laws in your physical world. Rather, by "law," we mean that which is absolute, or that which is governed strictly by the nature of the universe. Firstly, we must point out that All-That-Is, which constitutes the universe and all that exists within it, is composed entirely of pure love energy. All that which exists is made up of an energy so divine and absolute that nothing can penetrate it. You may be asking that if love is all there is, why then does hatred abound? We say to you that hatred is merely a misperception of the universal energy. In other words, hatred has arisen from one's inability to recognize the good within all things of the universe. Whenever hatred, in whatever form, is experienced, it is merely an illusion of the ego mind. Once you are able to raise your consciousness to a state above and beyond that of ego, you shall experience the blissfulness of pure love. Hatred, as with all illusions, is merely a matter of perception, and is therefore the result of your state of awareness.

Now, the first and foremost of the laws which govern the universe is that of attraction. When you recognize that all is energy, you will then recognize that energy acts as a magnetic force, drawing unto itself that which is like itself. Each thought you think has a vibration of its own which propels it out into the universe, attracting all other thoughts which are also vibrating at the same frequency. Your physical body can be likened to a transmitting and receiving device, and each thought you think constitutes your point of attraction. In other words, as you think, so shall you reap. Do you see the importance of understanding these laws?

For as you go about your days, barely noticing the direction your thoughts are being transmitted, you are constantly attracting into your experience all things which are in vibrational harmony with the nature of your thoughts. It is a very powerful position in which you stand, and it cannot be much fun unless you are aware of the rules of the game, so to speak. But, as you begin to understand the laws of the universe and the way in which they apply to you, you shall begin to utilize them consciously, rather than unknowingly, thereby molding your life experience into all that you want it to be. No longer shall you run around blindly bumping into walls that, in reality, are not there in the first place. Instead, you will learn to utilize your thoughts and the powers of the universe to create all your hearts' desires, as was your intent when you first donned physicality.

The second most powerful law (one is not really more powerful than another, merely utilized more often) is that of allowance or acceptance, which means that by allowing others to be as they want to be, you are, in essence, also allowing yourself to be what you want to be. By doing so, you are perpetuating freedom, and this, dear souls, is what it's all about. Through your free will, you have been given the freedom to be and do and have whatever you want. But at the same time, you must be willing to allow others the same freedom. This is the reasoning behind the separation of which we've spoken, for in this separating or dividing into segments, the universe (or God) simultaneously is able to experience many more realities than would be possible as a limitedly-focused Whole. The most freeing thing you can do for yourself is to release the notion that all others must be like you, and that they must have and desire the same things you do, for if that were the case, there would be no diversity, and without diversity, there would be no growth. You are each an aspect of the universe, utilizing your current personalities in order to experience life from various angles.

Free yourself from the bonds of illusion which say that you are separate from one another and you will simultaneously be allowing yourself to experience all facets of life in a much more knowledgeable, joyful manner. You are experiencing life through different bodies and different personalities, but we say to you that you are of one Mind. This smorgasbord of personalities is the true meaning of omnipresence, you see. God is everywhere, and He/It accomplishes this by expressing Him/Itself as that of you and that of your neighbor, as well as that of a bird and a rock and a tree. *Allow, allow,* children, and the universe will benefit greatly. Another important law for you to understand is that of sequence. No thing happens within your linear framework of time. There is no backward or forward, past or future, there is only *now*. If you feel you are going nowhere in life, realize that there is no such place; there is only *now-here*. We can assure you that you are adding unto the growth of the universe, no matter how useless you may feel. All things merely *are*, and all circumstances happen in sequence within the universal plan, rather than within your limited perceptions of time and space. You exist here in your physical body at this time, but you also exist amidst numerous other realities that you are not aware of consciously.

The universe is in a perpetual state of growth, and you, as aspects of the universe, are the impetus behind this growth. We cannot stress this point enough. Without your willingness to explore the far reaches of Mind, there would be no growth, and certainly no Earth school. For this, we commend you.

As we've said before, there are no time restrictions upon anything, and you have an eternity to "get it right," so to speak. All that which you perceive as past history upon the Earth plane exists now within the eternal structure of the universe. Picture a movie in which those involved in the making of the movie cut and edit the film, dropping the parts they don't like onto the cutting room floor and inserting new segments into the slots they've opened until they finally get it right. The Truth is pretty much the same thing. All your "nows" exist simultaneously in the present moment, which enables you to move in and out of each reality as you choose, adding or deleting new knowledge as you see fit. You do this all the time, dear ones, you are just not consciously aware of it. Begin to replace your harsh concept of linear time with the gentler concept of forever and you shall eliminate much fear upon your planet.

These three laws cover a broad range of information which will serve to advance the consciousness of humankind. There are many more laws which we will gladly tell you about later. For now, we hope we have painted a clearer picture of Truth; one that will enable you to seek joy as you are going about your seeming day to day strife. For there is no greater intent, from your higher perspective, than that of seeking joy and fully accepting it into each of your life experiences.

You are always speaking about "coming home." What does this mean?

When we refer to "Home," we mean that highest state of consciousness, of awareness, which many of you call "Heaven." In your true state of being, Heaven is where you reside, and it is for this reason that we refer to it as Home. Many of you may ask, *"But why would I ever choose to leave Home?"*

We say that you chose to leave Home, that state of all-knowing, in order to expand the universe to a state of even greater knowing, and for this you are to be commended. You see, dear ones, when you donned your physical bodies, you did so with the intention of expanding God's knowledge to a point which has never before been attained. You could say that you are on the cutting edge of thought, for as you interact with one another upon this physical plane, each thought and action offers the entire universe an opportunity to expand its knowledge in many directions. The universe is in a state of perpetual expansion, and this is because souls like yourself have chosen to venture into the realms of the unknown with the intention of adding to the ever-growing pool of known reality, which constitutes All-That-Is.

When speaking in terms of your Higher-Self, we are referring to that all-knowing portion of yourself which resides forever in God's world, or Heaven. This part of yourself never leaves the higher state of light and knowledge; only a piece of your consciousness ventures forth into physical reality at any given time. Therefore, when we urge you to return Home, we are simply reminding you of your purpose for being here in the first place, which is to reconnect your present self with your Higher-Self, thereby bringing Heaven (God) to Earth. You see, your attempts here to do just that are merely the universe's way of expanding its knowledge of Itself. When you fully understand the nature of the universe, you will know that all things exist as pure thought amidst the Universal Mind (another synonym for God), and you will also see that the expansion of which we speak is simply the stretching of thought. The only way to stretch or expand thought is by exploring the far reaches of Mind, such as interacting upon a physical plane.

The Earth was formed from the thought that asked: "What would it be like to exist in a reality in which all things were physical, whereas I could manipulate my thoughts in a way that they would become manifest as part of my physical reality?" And off you went to explore this thought further by interacting within it. Your main objective here is to eventually raise the awareness of who you are to such a degree that the Earth itself will be able to exist within the heavenly realms as a place, or rather a state, to go simply for the enjoyment of it. The Bible speaks of the Earth being created in darkness, devoid of all light (knowledge), and this is what we are referring to here. It is your chosen job as beings of light, to bring the light that you are to the Earth plane through your interactions within it. Again, heaven on Earth is the goal, and it shall be realized. You have expended much energy and put forth great effort toward making this dream a reality, and you will be greatly rewarded for your efforts. However, we must point out that the true reward comes not in the completion of a goal, but in the process of reaching the goal.

In your human state of becoming, of expansion, you have taken great strides toward recognizing who you truly are. Therefore, the "becoming" is the most beneficial aspect of the entire evolutionary process. You could say that humanity is learning to become as Christs, or co-creators with God. You must remember, however, to enjoy this physical experience, for it is only in your enjoyment of it that your goals will be actualized.

Truly, Home is where the heart is. It is a state of all-knowing (wisdom), of peace, of love, of pure bliss, to which each of you is striving to return with the Earth plane in tow. The highest part of yourself resides within this state permanently, and each of you has access to all the knowledge of the universe through your intuition, which is generated by the energy of your heart. How do you connect with this highest part of Self? You need only sit quietly and ask that it be so, and *hear* the answers as they stream from your heart and into your current state of consciousness. It is that simple. "Ask and ye shall receive." You always receive, we might add, but you do not always hear. There is no time as you know it, and therefore no time limit upon the aforementioned goal. However, the sooner you come to the full realization of your true place in the grand scheme of things, the sooner you shall rejoin God in the state of eternal bliss, of Heaven, of Home, and no longer shall you wallow in presumed darkness. See you there, dear children of the Earth.

Define Consciousness.

Consciousness is that part of yourself which allows you to be aware of your surroundings. It's the part of you that thinks, feels, and shows emotion. It is a link in the universal chain of life. When God created each of you, he did so with His mind, which is the same as consciousness. You exist as an aspect of Mind and are able to perceive yourself and all that around you via the conscious part of Mind. In other words, without consciousness you would not be aware of your state of existence.

Consciousness allows you the opportunity to change your mind at will. There are various states of consciousness, and therein lies the reasoning behind various realities. When the ego thinks in terms of realities, it often sees reality as only that which can be seen, felt, heard, or smelled by the physical senses. However, we say to you that there is much more to reality than meets the human eye. You perceive only that which your consciousness has willed you to perceive.

For instance, when you journeyed to the Earth plane, you willed your state of consciousness to be aware of and compatible with the Earth state of consciousness. However, even while existing upon the Earth plane, you can always choose to alter your state of consciousness to one more conducive to that of Truth, if you so desire. In Truth, you are each perfect, whole beings capable of creating and expanding the universe at will. However, there are parts of you, aspects of your consciousness, which see themselves as less than worthy of this inheritance. In other words, there is a portion of your self that still has trouble grasping reality, accepting your inherited Divinity.

The conscious portion of your being is capable of playing tricks on itself by telling you that you are not worthy of the riches of the Kingdom. Or, it may say that you cannot possibly be one with the Father, since you are capable of perceiving yourself as separate. Albeit, this constitutes a very minute portion of the Whole, but it nevertheless needs to be corrected so that all aspects of the life-governing force, or God, can be reunited as a perfected Whole. When this reunion occurs, each portion of the Whole (which constitutes each of you in human form), will know your worthiness beyond a shadow of doubt, and you shall accept the jeweled crowns of the Father without hesitation.

So you see, dear ones, there are many aspects of that which you call

God, and you are each a portion thereof. You are working diligently, seeking higher consciousness in order to fully understand yourself and your true nature. Even as we speak, you are busily exploring the nature of consciousness through your willingness to entertain life in the human form. Consciousness can then be said to be the mind aspect of the universe. It is the all-encompassing life-force which permeates all things. It is the aspect of yourself which says to you that you are unworthy, as well as that part of you which knows your full potential. We would define consciousness as your current state of being, of knowing, of becoming, for it determines, at all times, where you shall reside. By this, we mean that if you were to experience "hell," this would be because of your state of consciousness, which would include belief in such a place. Change your state of consciousness or mind and you shall simultaneously change your life experience. Ask your heart to guide you to the proper state of consciousness, enabling you to soar into the Heaven state of awareness to reclaim your crowns. Know that we are forever here (in our home within your heart), to offer assistance and all you need do in order to perceive us is change your state of mind, thereby altering your conscious perceptions.

CHAPTER THREE

Free Will Versus Predestination

"Never are you the victim of happenstance, but rather the creator of circumstance."

"Your life cannot be lead in any direction other than the way your thoughts are pointing."

The Apostles

How can free will and predestination exist at the same time?

Although our one great Father has indeed fashioned a road map or a blueprint which leads toward ultimate enlightenment, your free will is intact at all times. All things in this grand and glorious universe are one, and this includes you, dear souls. You are one with the ultimate Source, the Creator, for you are his creation. Thus, you also share in the delight of mapping out, so to speak, the evolutionary processes which unfold within each reality. So you see, dear ones, free will and predestination exist simultaneously, and you are the sole (Soul) creators of each. You designate your paths through predestination and carry them out through free will. We know this may cause some confusion; therefore let us offer an analogy: Picture yourself as part of an integrated universe, aspects of the Source Creator. See yourselves as mighty creators who, through your own thoughts, brought all things into being. Realize that your thoughts created the Earth plane as a place, or rather a state to go in order to seek greater understanding of your true nature.

Once the Earth plane was formed, you then had to map out, in general terms, the direction the Earth was going to take. Part of you then decided to don physicality to explore the exquisiteness of it firsthand, while the "rest" of your self chose to remain in the non-physical dimension, which is often referred to as the Soul, or the Higher-Self. This way, only a portion of you (which is your current personality), is focused in physical reality at any given time, while the remainder of your "self" stayed behind so that you may stay connected to and receive guidance from your higher state of being. In actuality, you are never disconnected from the Source; you only *think* you are.

Therefore, your Higher-Self, with whom you remain forever connected, retains full memory of the "map" or "blueprint" you laid out for yourself before journeying to Earth, and it works diligently to keep you focused on your Earth-life purposes. However, your free will is always intact, and therefore, many humans may find themselves choosing paths that are less conducive to Truth. The ego's enticements are cunning indeed, and you must learn to listen to your heart––your direct connection to the Source––in order to keep yourself on the proper path. We must point out that it is quite all right for you to stray or choose another path, but it is only when you find yourself in utter darkness and confusion that we wish to intervene, for we do not care to see our brothers and sisters of the earth suffering illusory pain.

We hope we have offered a clearer picture of Truth so you can see exactly how it is that you have created, through your free will, your entire life experience. You are not puppets with strings that are pulled by something outside yourself, as your notion of predestination might suggest. No, you are grand creators, aspects of the Whole, who have fashioned this place called Earth for yourselves, complete with road maps and blueprints, as a means of exploring and thereby understanding yourself more fully. You created the Earth and you designed the way you wanted it to unfold through the process of evolution. And you, through your thoughts and actions each day, decide whether to follow the plan or to create new ones. You do it all, dear ones. It is up to you, for no one but you creates your experience. Predestination is nothing more than the result of your free will. You may choose to traverse in any direction you wish. However, the more knowledgeable you are regarding your true purpose, the smoother your paths shall be.

Follow your heart, dear ones, and use your free will to bring yourself and your planet to the state of eternal bliss with as little confusion as possible.

You are always saying that we are on our proper paths in life, yet it seems we're being encouraged to "wake up" in order to choose another path. Isn't this contradictory?

Again, you do indeed have free will, and therefore you are on your chosen path at all times. You have created this "schoolroom" called Earth in order to learn more about yourself. However, from our vantage point, we can see that the problems arose when mankind ventured too far into the depths of the ego state of self-centered consciousness, which has caused you to become entrenched within the parameters of illusory darkness. And within this illusion of darkness, you believe you are experiencing pain in the form of hatred, envy, famine, war, and so on. While it is never our intent to encourage you to relinquish your free will, it *is* our intent to assist those of you who have found yourselves trapped within this illusion by throwing you life support in the form of knowledge. You need not suffer, dear ones, in order to learn a lesson. If the illusion of darkness is what you have consciously chosen for your Earth-school lessons, then so be it. But from our viewpoint, we know that it is oftentimes chosen inadvertently rather than intentionally, and it is this we are attempting to rectify. We hope to encourage those of you who are unintentionally wallowing in pain and darkness to rise above the illusory state of ego-centered consciousness so that you may find the joy and harmony that dwells within your being. This state of joy and harmony, of bliss, is what you call Heaven. It is already yours, dwelling within you, waiting to be tapped. This is precisely what Jesus meant when he said "The Kingdom of Heaven is within you." Seek no more outside yourself, dear peoples of the Earth, for the heaven you seek is within your heart at this moment. You need only awaken to the truth of which we speak in order to joyously and knowingly create a happier existence for yourself. Once this has been accomplished, you will have truly found yourself and there will be no more need for the delusional, fear-based limitations you've unerringly imposed upon yourselves.

What does "let go and let God" mean? Does this mean we have to surrender our free will?

There comes a time for all species that exist anywhere in the universe to begin opening their eyes and allow the Truth to penetrate their consciousness. The "Truth," of course, is that of Oneness. Many of you may be saying "But we've heard enough about Oneness—now tell us how it works." That, dear ones, is precisely what we are here to do, for the time is right upon the Earth plane for all to awaken and raise the level of collective consciousness to a state more conducive to that of Truth. In all fairness, we understand your need to hold onto that which seems safe, such as the ego state of mind, for that is all humankind has known for some time. However, to release your hold on the ego, you must trust in the Divine

Plan, knowing full well that what God has in store for you is always for the better-ment of all.

The Truth is coming to the peoples of Earth in unprecedented wavelengths. By this, we mean that humankind has risen in consciousness, via evolution, to a state which will allow the greater penetration of Truth. How then do you let go and let God? This is done merely through your intentions. In other words, you need only be willing to surrender to the will of our Father, and it shall be so. You might ask "What happens if I want to change my mind later on," or "Does this mean I'm surrendering my own free will?" You each have free will at all times and are, therefore, free to choose for yourself as you see fit.

However, know too that when all is said and done, when the last soul has come full circle, so to speak, to the state of highest awareness, then each of you will have surrendered your will fully in order for this exaltation to occur. If it seems to you then that free will is redundant, we say that Thy will *is* your will, for you and God are one and the same. The only will you are surrendering is that of falsity; i.e., the ego. For apparent reasons, God has given each of His children, all of whom are aspects of Himself, His own free will in order for the expansion to come about, which serves to enhance your understanding of that which God is. All things in existence are God, you included, and all things are constantly dividing and subdividing within themselves in order to reach the point of all-knowing and all-understanding.

You see, when you began your adventures as an aspect of God, you did so with much trepidation. "How can I possibly be as God," or "How can I ever live up to such expectations?" you asked. You doubted yourself and your ability to co-create. Thus is the reason for your current dilemmas. It is only because you have disallowed God's will to be your own will that you have been able to loose yourself, so to speak, from the Divine Source, thereby feeling lost. Because you felt unworthy of your inherent Divinity, you sought to prove to yourself that which you already are. You are perfect; you just don't know it. You are God; you just refuse to accept it. You are inheritors of the Kingdom, you just fail to recognize this fact. Your will *is* God's will, you have merely forgotten it. Therefore, when we speak of surrendering your will to God's will, we are not speaking of giving up anything. Quite the contrary. We are encouraging you to reclaim something which is already yours merely by allowing it to be so. The next time you're sitting alone attempting to make sense of all this, realize that by surrendering to God's will, you are in no way giving up anything––you, in fact, are gaining everything. Recognize the Divinity within you and thereby freeing yourself to accept all the riches of the universe; these are your rights of inheritance. The moment you awaken and begin to truly love yourself, deeming yourself worthy, shall be the precise moment there will be a unification of wills. Your will and God's will shall merge in your mind, for it is only your mind which needs adjustment in order to see that the two wills have been and always will be, in reality, one and the same.

We often find ourselves in situations like car accidents, in which we seem to be caught off-guard. Are events such as these pre-planned and therefore inevitable, or can we change our plans to avoid accidents?

This is a good question, for it allows us the opportunity to explain the extent of your abilities to create. Firstly, you do indeed create as you go, for that is the sole purpose for which you have chosen this physical lifetime. However, you did journey into this physical plane with a road map of sorts, a general blueprint, which would serve to keep you in line with your highest intent. Time, in reality, does not consist of linear constraints. Therefore, the "pre-planning" and the "creating as you go" aspects of time are really one and the same.

Now, when one of the Earth plane finds him or herself in a horrible car crash or some other accident, that person oftentimes looks for someone other than themselves to blame, for that is the way the ego works, you see. To the ego-mind, all things exist outside of self and all events are random and chaotic. Therefore, when one finds him or herself involved in some type of mishap, he or she oftentimes feels confused and ambushed by a stroke of bad luck. "What did I do to deserve this?" you might ask. Or you might say, "I was just at the wrong place at the wrong time." Such notions could not be farther from the truth, since in reality, all circumstances in which you find yourself enmeshed were created by you and for you as a means to a higher purpose. All things serve to perpetuate the Higher-will, the Truth, and no thing in this wonderful, grand universe is random, dear ones. You only think it is, which is part of the illusion of separateness. Your lives here are meant to be taken no more seriously than that of a play in which each of you has designated roles to carry out. Begin to see yourself as nothing more than an actor in a play with the desire to bring forth the truth of light and love to your planet. When the play is over and your role is complete, you shall once again return Home, shedding your costume, your physical body, along the way.

Now that we have established that no thing is random, we can conclude that all things which occur in your daily lives, including accidents, occur deliberately. You might say, "I would never intentionally put myself or another in jeopardy; therefore, how can I deliberately create an accident?" Firstly, we must point out that at no time are you unsafe, for in reality, nothing can harm the real "you." When seen from our broader perspective, you realize that death does not exist and pain of any kind is but illusion.

The real you exists eternally, forever safe within the strong arms of the universe. You may not be consciously aware of the road map you've laid out for yourself, but your Higher-Self is aware and serves to guide you along your intended path. All things which come into your experience, whether pleasant or unpleasant, are clearly brought forth by your higher intent, your desire to serve a purpose. You are, at all times, reading from your script in the play called life.

Once your current role here is complete, you shall find yourself entering other life experiences equipped with a much broader perspective, and you shall chuckle at the seriousness with which you took this physical life experience. Lighten up and enjoy the ride, for your efforts are truly assisting in the exaltation of your planet. No longer fear that a thing will catch you off-guard, for in the truest sense, from your higher perspective, you are well aware of what is to take place within your current Earth-school journey.

It may seem as if we have painted a strict picture of the lessons that are to take place in your lives, but this is not so. It is not our intent to make you feel as if you consciously have no power over your own life situations.

At all times do you hold the key to your own future, and you can choose to alter your circumstances any time you so desire.

Two paths to higher learning always exist: the easy path and the more difficult one, and you choose these paths according to the nature of your thoughts. If your thoughts are predominantly negative, then your Higher-Self takes this to mean that you are thereby choosing the more difficult path. If your thoughts are positive, your Higher-Self will see to it that you arrive at the same conclusions, only much more gently. Therefore, we would urge you to set forth your positive intentions at the beginning of each day, thereby allowing your Higher-Self to know your intent to choose the easy path Home, and it will be done. Our main goal is to enable you to see that no matter what the circumstances surrounding your life, you are, in reality, safe from harm. Nothing can hurt you, dear ones, and the sooner you recognize this fact, the sooner you will begin to lighten up and enjoy this physical life experience, this play called Earth-life. No thing is random, and there is always a purpose to your pain. We implore you to rise above the ego state of pain and see yourself as a lighted love being filled with the Higher-Will, who has merely chosen to don a particular character or personality in order to carry out a certain role for the good of All. Remove the cloak of fear you are wearing and see yourself as eternal manifestations of All-That-Is, and you shall quickly come to the crossroads of Truth.

How can we learn to allow others to act in any way they please without allowing their actions to affect our lives?

Again, there is never a moment when you are not completely safe within the strong, nurturing arms of the universe. We know this may be difficult to understand for those of you who may have experienced some type of assault, but we must point out the truth to clarify this issue. *Never* does another come into your experience without your invitation. Now, you might say, "But I would never have invited a mugger or rapist into my experience." While we agree that you did not intentionally invite such a person into your life, you nevertheless invited them unintentionally or inadvertently via the thoughts and subsequent emotions that you offered to the universe.

Remember, dear ones, thought is energy, and like attracts like. Therefore, when you are offering thoughts of a negative nature or vibration to the universe, you are attracting all things within the universe which are of like vibration. For instance, you may not be thinking so much about being raped or mugged, but you have, through your negative vibration, opened yourself up to all other negative thought forms existing within the universe. By offering fear, for example, you attract those things into your experience which serve to compound your fears. This is the way the universe works. You are not experiencing bad things in your life as punishment for something you've done, but rather to amplify the power of your thoughts, your power as co-creator. You came forth into physical reality in order to learn more about the nature of the universe, which includes your own power as an aspect of All-That-Is. The best way to accomplish this is by exploring within a physical reality in such a way whereas your thoughts become manifest as part of your reality. The density of the Earth plane offers a cushion of time, so to speak, which allows you to redirect your thought patterns if need be to that which is more conducive to what you want. With each circumstance in your life, you are brought closer to the truth of who you are. The truth is that you are grand and glorious creators, beings of light, who are capable of producing all your hearts' desires with the power of your thoughts.

Your thoughts can be likened to a powerful magic wand that you wave about, creating all that which you desire, and sometimes that which you don't. Only through the recognition and full realization of your most awesome powers will you come to understand that it is *you* who create your world strictly by the nature of your thoughts. Physicality offers the greatest opportunities for the growth and realization of this fact by allowing you to experience the manifestation of your thoughts on a physical level. Life experiences teach——mere words do not. Allow your thoughts to become pure by offering only positive vibrations of love and harmony to the universe, and that shall be all you experience during this physical lifetime. This, dear souls, is what you are here to learn. All that exists is striving to overcome any aspects of illusion which say negativity exists, in order to create a universe filled with only peace, love, and harmony. This is the goal, and the only way to accomplish it is by living through each experience with full realization as to how it came about, so that you can begin creating for yourself only those things that you do want, rather than those things you don't want.

To summarize, we can say that allowing others to be and do as they please does not mean their actions have to affect you. You simply need not give your attention to what others are doing by focusing only upon what you want to experience, and their turmoil cannot touch you. You are each free to create in any way you see fit in order to learn a lesson or two about your true nature. If the illusion of negativity serves to bring you closer to the truth, then so be it. It is one's right to act any way he chooses, but that need not affect you. Once you can truly allow others their freedom, then you are in actuality allowing yourself the freedom to do as you please. Learn to give your attention only to the things you want––(never to what you don't want)––and that shall be all you experience. It is that simple. Live your life and allow others to live theirs. Then your paths will not meet anywhere in between unless you invite them to do so through the thoughts you think.

When you offer negative thoughts to the universe, you are, in essence, saying, "Bring more negativity unto me." It is the universe's job to respond to your commands, for you are the creator. On the other hand, when you offer positive thought vibrations, you are saying, "Bring unto me only that which is in harmony with who I truly am." There is much power in your thoughts, for they represent your point of attraction. The sooner you come to this realization, the sooner you shall find yourself living within the state of eternal bliss, and the dream of a perfect universe filled with only peace and love shall be realized.

Commend yourself for your efforts to bring this dream to fruition, for without your willingness to be here on this physical plane, interacting amidst the outer edges of thought, there would be no growth within the universe. You are as mighty warriors seeking to abolish all aspects of illusion and negativity, and for that, dear ones, we are most appreciative. Respect yourself and each other and the work you do here, for you are truly adding unto the knowledge of the Whole with each interaction that you participate in, whether you are aware of it at the time or not.

CHAPTER FOUR

Illuminating the Bible's Messages

"God exists as the highest potential state of being, consisting of absolute peace, love, and bliss, to which humanity is striving."

The Apostles

When Was the Earth First Formed?

When the Earth was first formed, it was formed from thought, as are all things in existence. Therefore, it can be said that all that which exists does so within the realm of thought, or as a thought form——a dream, you might say. This is the reason why God, the one great energy Source, is often referred to as Universal Mind, for that is precisely where all things—— including yourself——reside: within the mind of God. Now that we have clarified that issue, let us move on to tackle the tougher issue, which is that all things were created in a linear fashion with some sort of attached history.

This type of linear thinking was created by the ego's need to see all things as separate from itself. In Truth, all things——the Earth included—— merely are. Therefore, it is impossible to place an exact time and date upon the formation of the Earth. In reality, the time and space aspects of earth-life do not exist. However, we can say that the Earth has been in existence since the Universal Mind conceived it via the power of thought.

The Universal Mind is a creative energy which constantly expresses Itself through the thoughts It thinks, and your Earth is merely one of those thoughts. The idea of forming the Earth plane arose from the Spirit's desire to expand itself further by recognizing its true nature (Spirit means those aspects of God which include yourselves). The Earth was first formed, in your terms, many millennia ago, devoid of all light, and it was Spirit's job to venture forth into this dream in order to bring light unto the darkness. This is a great challenge to you from the perspective of your True-Self, and when this task has been fulfilled, the Earth and all things of it shall return Home only to seek, once again, another angle from which to expand awareness.

Therefore, it can be said that the Earth is as old as a thought and as new as a dream. How many of you are able to put linear constraints upon your own dreams? Do you dream a dream and say "That was yesterday's dream," or "April 1994's dream" as it flits through your consciousness? Rather, when you have manifested a particular dream within your own thought system, you tend to carry that dream with you, clenched tightly to your heart, until it is realized. You are unable to dismiss it so easily as to say "Oh, there goes last year's dream again" as it crosses your mind.

Your dreams exist within your heart eternally and in the Now. The same holds true for the "Earth dream" which is forever held tightly within the bosom of the Universe. Each thought and expression of Divinity exists simultaneously amidst the eternal Now, but to appease the egos of your world, we will agree with your notion that the Earth is multi-billions of years old. However, in Truth, it is as young as is Now. We understand your need to pinpoint exact dates, but we feel this would only compound the confusion we are attempting to alleviate.

From the ego's viewpoint, the Earth is as old as it *seems* to be. However, from our vantage point, it merely exists within the eternal Now, with no past or future smudging the present. No matter what the age of your planet, all you need be concerned with is Now. Ask yourself "What am I doing Now to help bring my planet Home," or "What can I do Now to heal the Earth of its woes?" These are the true issues, dear ones, not whether humans existed before dinosaurs or vice versa. Expend your energies on things beneficial to the Whole. Offer only love to your planet and peace shall follow. Know that in your true state of being, you are privy to all the answers you seek, and many of these answers are available to you now, if only you would learn to go within and listen to your heart. Your heart energies are chock-full of knowledge, for your heart is your direct link Home. Hone these energies and much fear and confusion shall be wiped from the face of the Earth.

What is Meant by the Alpha and the Omega?

The Alpha and the Omega simply mean All-That-Is. This expression was meant to imply the non-beginning and the non-ending of all things in existence. In Truth, there is no beginning and no ending to anything; there is only "Being-ness." It is only through the illusions within your limited ego-mind that you have been able to place time constrictions on anything. Know that in Truth, there is no time or space. God is all there is. God is ever-present and omnipresent. God is the energy source which permeates everything and sustains life forevermore. God is also who *you* are. God is the rock and the tree, as well as the bird upon the tree branch and the roots beneath the tree. So, we can deduce that *you* are the Alpha and the Omega. *You* exist beyond time and space, *you* are ever-present and omnipresent amidst the eternal bosom of the universal Whole. Begin to see yourself as the Divine being you truly are; you are one with the Father who created you. Open your heart to this fact and all the presumed mysteries of the universe shall unfold neatly within your lap. Know that all the answers you seek, dear ones, are already within your very own being, waiting to be exposed and recognized by your conscious ego self. Your intuition is your direct link to this vast store of knowledge. Hone your intuitive skills and uplift your spirits to a state of higher awareness. Only then will you be homeward bound and your greater awareness shall make the Earth journey much sweeter indeed.

What is Meant by the Second Coming of Christ?

When the man known to your world as Jesus walked the Earth, there was a great need for humanity to come to grips with reality, so to speak. Jesus was sent to carry a message to the peoples of the Earth, and that message was: Go within and live from the heart, for there lies the seat of your being. Jesus plainly told them that God was not outside themselves, but rather that God existed within their hearts as their highest potential state of being. However, many chose not to hear this message of Truth, thereby creating the need for history to repeat itself. The Second Coming of Christ does not refer to Jesus the man. Rather, it is another attempt to allow the peoples of the Earth an opportunity to find themselves, to realize their God-potential. There are numerous paths one can choose to return Home, and some of these paths are not nearly as pleasant as others. It is up to you, humanity as a whole, which path you choose. You will get here one way or another, but we would urge you to open your hearts and seek the truth, for it is far better this way in the long run.

Again, Christ Consciousness was not given only to the one man known as Jesus. Rather, it is within each and every one of you, just waiting to be tapped. The Christ Consciousness is a heavenly state of mind waiting within your heart for the opportunity to express itself through your physical being. Thus, the second coming will not be that of a man in human form, per se, sweeping down upon the Earth, plucking up those who are worthy and then retreating back to the heavens, leaving the rest of humanity dumbfounded and brokenhearted. No, dear ones, this is a false picture. The Second Coming of Christ is simply the dawning of a new era, a spiritual unfolding which will usher in the Truth for the peoples of the Earth. The time is right, the second coming is already under way, and each of you is a grand part of this evolutionary process.

So, it can be said that the second coming has already stolen its way onto your planet like a thief in the night. Contrary to what many religious leaders tell you, you need only look about in order to see that no one is missing and no single sinner is left dumbfounded. Thus it can be said that Christ has already come and you are each in the midst of the second coming. Search for this truth within you, grab it, and hold onto it for dear life, for it is truly the catalyst which will serve to bring humanity Home. Peace be with you, children, and remember to sit up and take notice as the Christ Consciousness knocks at the door to your heart.

What have you to say to those who want to clothe God in human form?

Many in your world have a difficult time accepting that human-ness is not at the core of your being. Albeit, you are indeed human at this particular time, but you are a much broader, expanded being than you perceive yourself to be. When God created humanity, He did so in His image, meaning that you contain the potential within you to be as God, to radiate only the peace, love and knowledge of the higher state of being. (Image also means imagination, to imply that all things in existence were created as a thought within the One Mind of God.) God is the ever-expanding source of creative light from which each of you spawned. God is love energy, and this love energy is all there is: therefore God is all there is. God exists *as* the highest state of being, of mind, which consists of absolute peace, love, joy, and harmony; and as fragments of this single creative Source, you each have the capacity to unleash the God potential within you in order for peace, love, and harmony to be expressed through your physical self. This is precisely the goal for those of you living upon the Earth at this time, for as you allow this Source energy to be expressed through you––which is accomplished by your expanded awareness of Truth——your ultimate goal of Heaven on Earth shall be realized.

Humans have oftentimes felt the need to put a human form upon that which is nonphysical, for that is all you have known. But in reality, you are not physical. Your true essence is that of non-physical, creative energy. You are grand and glorious energy beings. Energy cannot be seen, touched, or heard by your physical senses unless there is a physical conduit which allows you to perceive it, such as that of a light bulb. The same thing applies to your True-Self, which requires the use of a physical body so that Self may be perceived in this physical time and place.

So, God exists as the highest state of non-physical being, of mind, to which all is striving. Where does thought fit into all this? It is precisely this: Energy takes on many forms, and one of them is consciousness, which is the ability to focus thought energy into a specific arena. As you utilize your abilities to think or focus thought energies, you are tapping into the core energy (God), and together you create worlds. Thus, the words "mind," "thought," and "energy" can be used interchangeably.

Now, when you feel the need to personify that which you call God, realize that this simply is the way the ego was designed——it perceives all things as separate from self and all things as like unto self. A good example would be that of Santa Claus, for Christmas represents the spirit of giving, of peace, of love, of harmony——all those things attributed to the God state of mind. Yet, humanity felt the need to clothe even the spirit of Christmas with that of a jolly old man in a red suit, you see. We are certainly not discouraging this practice, for we encourage anything that serves to make Truth real for you. However, we want you to understand that what is meant to be taken metaphorically should not be taken literally, for this practice tends to compound your confusion. You know that Santa Claus is not real: He is merely a figment of your imagination that was conjured up by the ego's need to place a human face upon a non-physical spirit of being-ness. All that which you perceive as real exists within your mind. It is then projected outward into your experience. *Your entire life is the outward projection of your internal beliefs.*

When you created the Earth and all the beliefs that go with it, you simply took the Truth and turned it upside down. The Earth and all its illusions can be said to be the exact opposite of Truth. Why would you do such a thing? Simply for the experience of it, for the exhilaration of coming forth into this physical time and place of contrast in order to expand consciousness to a point it has never gone to before. In the process of experiencing contrast of the highest degree, you are stimulating yourself to further creativity through your interaction within it.

Therefore, if you believe reality is only that which is physical, you need to look at the opposite side of the coin and there you shall find Truth. In reality, all things are non-physical and intangible as is energy, and energy is all there is. It is only through the process of focusing thought energy that one is able to funnel the field of pure potentiality into seemingly physical manifestations. The next time your ego attempts to put a face on that which you call God, realize that in reality, God has no name and no face. At the same time, God is every name and every face, for God is omnipresent. In other words, the Source Creator is expressing Itself as each and every life form upon your plane. It can be likened to a game of hide-and-seek wherein God hides Himself within your very being, offering you opportunities to seek and eventually reunite this higher part of Self with your physical self.

Although God is without name and form, He is simultaneously every name and every face which has ever been and will ever be. If you still insist upon putting a face on that which you call God, may we suggest you use your own, for as you stand gazing at your image in the mirror, realize that God is within that image, waiting patiently to be recognized. God is the eternal-ness, the All-That-Is-ness of being, and this, dear souls, is all there is. Nothing exists outside this highest state of being, (although in some instances it may appear otherwise, and this is what we call "illusion").

To allow God, your highest potential, to be expressed through you, you need only open your heart and allow the love of who you are to spill forth. This is the key. There are no shortcuts to God, for God is a process, a realization or awareness of Truth. God cannot be taught through history books or by teachers; this state can only be *realized*, which is the precise reasoning behind your humanness. Nothing you can possibly do would be incorrect in the eyes of God, for all you experience serves to add unto the growth of the Whole. The next time you gaze upon your image in the mirror, choose to see yourself as God, as the spark of creative consciousness that you are, and you shall be much closer to achieving the ultimate goal of humanity, which always has been and always will be Heaven (God) on Earth.

Remember that God exists *as* the highest possible state of being, of awareness, of mind, and once you've realized this fact, no longer will you feel the need to personify and thereby limit that which is eternal and Whole.

What Do Biblical References to "Paradise" Imply?

Paradise—the very word has a ring to it, does it not? When Jesus spoke of Paradise, he was referring to that state of consciousness commonly known among the peoples of Earth as Heaven. The word "Paradise" simply means a resting place of great beauty, and we can assure you this describes the true Home that awaits each of you. All you need do to experience this heavenly Home is to seek it, and it shall be yours—we cannot stress this point enough. But due to free will, you always have the option of either choosing Paradise or denying it.

It seems silly, does it not, that one would intentionally deny Paradise? Yet this is precisely what happens each and every time one makes a choice to remain in darkness. The only place darkness exists is within the parameters of the ego-centered mind, and since the ego itself is not real, in reality, darkness does not exist. Paradise then can be said to be the state of mind to which all is striving. This state of mind consists of perfection and wholeness, abundance and beauty, peace, love, harmony, and good will—all the attributes of God. The one thing Paradise does not consist of, however, is ego.

You see, dear ones, when you donned physicality and trekked to the Earth, you did so with one thought in your mind, which was to bring yourself and your planet fully Home. By this, we mean that blissful state of mind which exists within you as a potential called Paradise (or Heaven, or God, among other names). By "fully," we mean all aspects of your soul, which includes all of the various personalities you have ever been and ever will be. The goal of the entire universe is to expand its awareness through each living entity and each incarnation in a way which will allow for the unveiling of Paradise within the entire framework of life. It will be wondrous when all aspects of the Whole join together in unison with nothing but Paradise on their minds. The universe (or God) works in constant forward motion, devoid of all space and time concepts, in order to expand and fulfill the one desire of the Source Creator, which is to have all His children Home again with the full realization that Paradise is where you belong.

Truly, the only thing you have set out to learn on your earthly journeys is that you do belong in Paradise, and that Paradise belongs in you. If you only knew, dear children, what you were missing by not allowing yourself to be fully present in Paradise, never again would you stray. It is our hope to assist our lost brothers and sisters of the Earth in finding your way back home to Paradise. It is the only place worthy of such kings and queens as yourselves. Awaken now and allow the universe to guide you to your true state of being via your heart connection. Paradise can only be found within—never outside of—yourself. Humanity has searched for Paradise outside of self for eons, but to no avail. The moment humankind begins to search in the right place, Paradise shall be yours forevermore.

What's the Real Story of Adam and Eve, and the Garden of Eden?

When you are perusing the Bible, we must remind you to read between the lines so you can glean the true meaning behind each parable. We say "parable," for that is precisely the way much of the information in the Bible is relayed. Although this is an efficient means of getting across a message, it has, nevertheless, caused much confusion, because many have believed the information literally when it was meant to be taken metaphorically. First and foremost, we would encourage you to check your own heart before coming to a conclusion regarding any matter, for doing so will dispel any confusion.

With that thought in mind, let us tackle the question at hand: Adam and Eve did exist as an extension of the human race at the time when humans, as you know them, came to exist. In other words, humanity existed prior to Adam and Eve, but without the ego. As the ego came to be upon your planet, so too was the current human persona born. When humans first existed upon the Earth plane, they were capable of direct communications with the world of God, which resulted in complete awareness of one's true essence and purpose for being. In other words, humanity existed within a higher state of consciousness than that which is presently known, which meant that they knew exactly who they were and from where they hailed. Earlier humans were well aware that they had journeyed to Earth and donned physicality in order to complete a particular mission, which always served to awaken the collective consciousness of Earth.

This higher state of awareness existed for many millennia, but the need arose to make your journeys into physicality appear more separated from the Whole than was actually the case. Once this need, or better stated, this desire was realized, the ego was born. The ego was simply meant to be used as a tool, of sorts, which would offer you the opportunity to believe in separateness so you could expand upon thought. This was done because the evolutionary processes had, to that point, brought the Earth to a kind of standstill. So ego was born as a means to expand upon your earthly stint in a way which would allow greater understanding and growth in the long run. When those of the Earth who first experienced this new ego state of mind were offered options, the choice was made to venture toward the negative side of thought, which included the illusions of separateness and lack.

This was the parable which described Adam and Eve and the serpent in the Garden of Eden, and this same story is also depicted in the "Fall." It can then be said that Adam and Eve were not the first humans who existed upon the Earth, but rather the first ego-humans. When they decided to eat fruit from the tree of knowledge of good and evil, they thus made the decision that all humanity would believe in the illusions of separateness, lack, and negativity of any kind. This can be seen in the story of the fig leaf; whereas upon giving birth to the ego, the illusion of separateness took the form of shame. The shameful feeling one may experience when unclothed is the greatest proof of the belief in separateness, which has continued down through the ages.

As with all parables and metaphors, some fiction is mixed with fact to add more spice to the story. Speaking about the devil or serpents acting as tempters was merely one writer's way of putting a face upon the ego, thereby causing much confusion and speculation. Although this was not done intentionally, it is nonetheless the case.

There you have it, dear souls of the Earth, your portrait of Adam, Eve, and the Garden of Eden, wrapped up nicely and presented as Truth. Make no mistake that ego was indeed created for a reason. However, it has been allowed to run rampantly, going above and beyond its intended purpose. Also, keep in mind the Truth of Oneness. There is no single person upon whom the rest of humanity can lay the finger of blame concerning the decisions that have been made. Each of you is responsible for all actions that take place upon your planet, for you are each aspects of the same Creator, seemingly divided into separated fragments called individuals. By allowing the ego to continue its rampant course, you are contributing to the erosion of your planet as much as if you had eaten the fruit yourself. You must awaken now from your slumber and stop blaming others for all your ills. You need only look within yourself for the answers you seek. Allow your True-Self to reign, thereby disabling the ego's stranglehold over your senses. Put the ego, the illusion of separateness, in check, dear ones, and come Home, for there is no surer way to remain lost than following the forlorn ways of ego.

In the Book of Revelations, Armageddon, a horrible end for the Earth, is predicted. Is this inevitable?

As you know by now, there are many paths available to the peoples of the Earth, all of which lead homeward. In other words, you each have the covenant of free will bestowed upon you at all times, and you are therefore free to choose which path to traverse. You will get here one way or another, but it is up to you whether you choose the difficult path or the easy one. What you have referred to as Armageddon can be said to be the difficult path. How do you know which path you're choosing? You need only go within to find the easy path, which is laid out in your heart much like a map, available to be followed when you are ready to see it.

Let us return to the truth of Oneness: All things in the universe, including you, are connected to the one great Source many call God. It is this energy Source which sustains all through its never-ending flow of love.

The Earth itself is also comprised of this same energy source, thus making yourself one with the Earth as well as all things of it. The Earth is part of each of you, and the ills it experiences through abuse and neglect are, in turn, heaped upon yourself. When the Earth is treated with disrespect, its only recourse is to turn within itself in order to shed its outer layers and begin anew. This process could cause many cataclysms, for you reap what you sow. You must therefore be careful of the ways you treat your planet, since it can only take so much abuse. You must begin to realize that the Earth is an extension of yourself, acting out a particular part in the play called life. If it weren't for the cooperation of this aspect of yourself, there would be no Earth school, and for that alone you owe it much gratitude.

What does this have to do with your question? It is this: It can be said that the greatest threat to your planet at this moment is the lack of care given to it. You must take time to recognize your own Divinity, as well as that of the Earth's, thereby allowing for the lessons the Earth has to offer, but minus the tribulations. Awaken, children, and heed the Earth's cries. It is in great need of affection, and it is entirely up to you as individuals to recognize this need, thus bringing an overall healing to the state of affairs amidst your current reality.

Unless the ego's current rampage is stopped, there shall be much unnecessary suffering. Many egos of your world have felt the need to rule your entire planet by attempting to convert all of humanity to the beliefs of a particular religion. You need to awaken and listen to your heart, which will bring greater understanding of the true nature of things, thereby putting an end to this nonsense for good. No longer allow others, whether they be leaders of your churches or leaders of your countries, to lead you in ways contrary to your own heart. Learn to go within to seek proper guidance, for it can never be found outside yourself. Wake up and realize this fact, and the power you've handed over to certain ego-dominated leaders shall be rescinded——and their power shall then be no more than that of a light bulb. You each have the power of the universe within you, dear souls. The moment you collectively awaken to this truth will be the precise moment when Earth shall choose the easy path Home.

Armageddon will be known to you only if you allow it to be so. The choice is yours, dear ones. Reclaim your personal power, your Divinity, your birthright, thereby demanding that the egos of the world relinquish theirs.

There shall then be much peace known by the inhabitants of your planet, and your hearts shall rejoice with the realization that you have returned Home safely and without disaster—for this is truly the intended way.

Many people have taken Biblical references to the only begotten son to mean that Jesus was the one and only son of God. Can you clarify this issue?

When referring to the only begotten Son, can you not see how each and every one of you exists as the totality of the only begotten son, seemingly divided into separate individuals? To say that the man known as Jesus was the only begotten Son is simply the ego's way of perpetuating the illusion of separateness. And we would also like to add here for those of you concerned with the annihilation of your consciousness at some point in time, that as long as you perceive yourself to exist, no matter what the form, you can rest assured that your consciousness shall remain for eternity. A thought cannot be unthought once it has been launched. All thoughts exist as living, breathing entities; therefore, once the aspect of consciousness known as "you" was conceived, that aspect, or you, will remain forever as a spark of divinity with the capacity to create, as does God. All your seeming trials and tribulations simply serve to enhance your awareness of the true nature of your divinity.

Your interactions here are meant to bring you back to the realization that you have never been separate from Source, no matter how separate the ego may perceive the Self to be. Therefore, upon hearing references to the One Son, or the only begotten son of God, place yourself in the equation, for each of you exists as a piece of the One Son, displaying different aspects of one personality. Picture this: God, the Infinite Mind, conceived the Earth plane, upon which would dwell a species called humanity. With that initial thought was born the one Son, which constitutes all of humanity. Then, over the centuries, the One Son began to see himself as separate, and all things perceived as existing outside of self. Once the ego was born, all hell broke loose, so to speak, amongst the heavenly kingdom called Earth. The Earth then took a nose dive into the lower realms of existence (the Fall), for a species cannot coexist harmoniously within the higher planes without being fully aware of the truth of Oneness. So, as you go about your lives, you are working to raise the Earth's vibrations through your increasing awareness of Truth in order to bring the Earth plane back to its proper status amidst the heavenly spheres.

Thus we can conclude that Jesus the man was indeed the begotten Son of God, but so too are each of you in human form. Your only differences lie in your differing perspectives; you are each aspects of the One Son, viewing life from different vantage points within the one mind of God. And this, dear souls, is the meaning of omnipresence. God exists in His (Its) entirety within every point in space, which means that you each exist *as* God, full of God potential, waiting patiently within your very being to be expressed through you and as you. As aspects of the One Mind, you are each created equally as the Whole of God, and the seed of this truth lies within the energies of your heart. Without each and every perspective or personality upon your plane, the Whole would not be complete. Therefore, every one of you plays a grand role in bringing the awareness of Heaven to Earth.

The words you use to describe yourselves reflect your greater knowing of this truth. For example, the word "person" is meant to imply the **per**spective of the **son**, you see. The truth is hidden within every nuance of your earthly lives, for you designed it that way in the hope that you would not easily forget who you truly are. Pat yourself on the back for a job well done and know that at all times, you hold within yourself the key which will unlock the door to the heavenly realms. Awaken now, dear peoples, and hear us as we speak to you from our home within your heart. Hear the messages of the angelic spheres as we broadcast the truth to you. Know that all is one and one is all, united forever within the One Mind of God. Find the peace within yourself that is waiting to be expressed, and with it shall come the knowledge regarding your true place within the grand scheme of things. You *are* the universe in its entirety, dear ones. You *are* the Kingdom, and you *are* the power that will eventually bring unity to all aspects of the One Son who currently dwell upon the Earth as seemingly separate individuals. Once this evolutionary process has been completed, you shall have your Heaven on Earth and nevermore shall you sleep, dreaming about the illusion of separateness.

What did Jesus mean when he said, "Unless ye turn and become as children, ye shall not enter the kingdom of heaven"? (Matthew 18:3)

When Jesus said to the peoples of the Earth that one must become as little children before entering the kingdom of Heaven, he was referring, of course, to one's state of mind, for isn't that all there is? If you were to stand a child and an adult side by side and view them closely, you would see that their greatest differences lie not in their sizes, but rather in their demeanors. The child would be filled with life and spontaneity, while the adult would seem burdened by life, lacking spontaneity and joy. If the adults of your world would simply allow themselves to return to the playful state of childlike consciousness from which each of you emerged, you would find yourself much closer to Truth, and much closer to knowing the God-Self within. You must realize, dear ones, that the universe is a joyful, playful, spontaneous experience, and that in order to become as children, awakened to the child within you, you must lighten up and begin to enjoy your life experience, for that is why you created this wonderful place called Earth in the first place. You did not create it to subject yourself to pain and misery. Rather, you envisioned a playground of sorts, which would serve, through your interactions within it, to bring you closer to the truth regarding your true nature as eternal beings of light and love.

We oftentimes refer to the Earth as "Earth school," for this is precisely the case—you have "enrolled" yourself here so you may learn to become more perfect creators, creating only light and love. But it must be enjoyable or no true learning is derived. Thus, when Jesus uttered those words, He meant to imply that you must regress yourself to that childlike state of consciousness you had when you were younger which allowed you to express yourself joyfully, playfully, spontaneously, and fearlessly in order to know the state of Heaven. It is that simple, dear ones. Enjoy yourself, lighten up, and no longer allow the ego to tell you that life should be taken seriously. The entire universe is a playground, and we would encourage you to bring yourself to this same, playful state so that you may have your Heaven on Earth.

What is meant by, "As ye sow, so shall ye reap?"

This statement simply means that all thoughts are as seeds, and wherever the seeds of thought are planted, they shall eventually grow into something tangible. Oh, if you dear souls but knew the power you wield with your thoughts, you would quickly put an end to your current way of thinking. Alas, this is the problem, for humans have long refused to allow this one great truth into their psyches. Your thoughts *are things*, and the sooner you recognize this, the sooner you shall return Home to the higher states of awareness. Each time you think a thought, that thought is propelled out into the universe by an energy force, where it exists as a living, breathing creation. It is then drawn by magnetic force to other thoughts that are like unto it.

Like attracts like, as you say, so when you are constantly thinking negative thoughts, you are in turn attracting other negative thought forms into your experience. Then you oftentimes find yourself deluged with negativity and unaware that it was your own free will to think any thoughts you choose, which caused your predicament. But once you begin to realize that all you need do to attract the things you want into your life is to think positive thoughts, you shall then begin to create all your heart's desires. Fill your mind with positive thoughts and negative thoughts want nothing to do with you, you see, for negative thoughts are interested only in other negative thoughts. By focusing only upon that which is good, of God, you allow yourself to flow in harmony with Truth. Your life will then begin to turn direction and you shall find your days filled with joy and spontaneity, erasing the darkness of yesterday. Thus is the meaning of the phrase, "The truth shall set you free" for once the Truth is realized, you shall be free to enjoy this life experience by deliberately creating all your heart's desires. As we've stated before, thoughts are things, and energy follows thought. "But how can my thoughts be things when I am unable to see them," you might ask. Our answer is but you *do* see them. As you look about, you can see that your thoughts always manifest somewhere in your reality, whether or not you are aware of the process. The Earth plane is of a much denser nature than the higher planes, which means that before a thought can become manifest, it must first trudge through time. Each time you think a thought, that thought usually does not manifest as part of your reality for days, weeks, months, or sometimes years, depending upon the time it takes for you to allow it into your life.

On a plane with a higher vibrational frequency, your thoughts become manifest more quickly, usually instantaneously. You can see the benefit of the denser planes, such as Earth, wherein you are offered opportunities to become more perfect creators by watching your thoughts become things over a period of time. In essence you are here on this Earth plane to perfect your creative skills. We want you to go back through your life experiences and recognize that what we say is true. All that which you experience as your reality has been brought unto you by the nature of your thoughts. If your thoughts are negative, then so shall your experience be. If your thoughts are positive, then so shall your experience be. Thus, "As ye sow, so shall ye reap." Each thought you think is as a seed, and once planted, it is on its way toward sprouting into a creation. You are powerful creators, dear peoples of the Earth, and in order to bring yourselves and your planet Home, you must awaken to this truth. Begin to use your powers wisely by creating only peace and love upon your beautiful planet. Realize that you can have or be or do all you desire, for all your desires exist within you as potentials waiting to be created. It is you and only you who creates your life experience. Love yourself, love your neighbors, and love your planet by creating a harmonious world in which to dwell. Sow only peace, love, and kindness, dear ones, and that is all you shall reap.

What is meant by the phrase, "As above, so below?"

This phrase implies that all things in your world of form were crafted from the original, absolute state, which is that of Heaven, or God. In other words, your world is a mirror reflection of the higher, more refined world of God. Albeit, these higher realms do not contain the likes of ego, but that is the beauty of the Earth plane. For as you work to overcome such illusion, you are in the process of creating new heavens. As you journeyed forth to partake in the illusion of Earth-life, you knew by your very presence here, by your willingness to believe in illusion, that you would greatly advance the growth of the Whole.

As we speak of the importance of your missions here, we feel it is also necessary to explain the nature of your present state of being. Firstly, the Earth plane and all its natural beauty was fashioned from the great expanse of thought that constitutes the universe. In other words, there is something of everything ever created amidst your earthly world of form. Not all things are as of yet visible to the human eye, but nevertheless, they exist within the hearts of man as potentials. As you bring greater and greater technologies to fruition, you are merely dipping into this vast store of potential. And, we might add, if you are flabbergasted at the rapidity of your advancing technology, we can only say you haven't seen anything yet——the best is yet to come!

You have just begun the transitional evolutionary phase which will fully integrate the higher heavenly state of awareness with that of the Earth state of being, and you call this Heaven on Earth. This is a wondrous time to be physically focused, for as you participate within the shedding of illusion, you are simultaneously assisting in the unveiling of Truth upon your planet. There is no greater thrill than the realization and remembrance of who you truly are and your purpose for being human.

Now, in order to clarify the issue of the Earth mirroring its higher counterpart, we will attempt to assimilate for you a portrait of the nature of physicality. Envision your world as that of a holographic image which reflects the vibrational frequency of the Heaven state of consciousness. As science is proving, all that which exists is made of pure energy. Many refer to this energy as pure love energy and that is correct, for all things of this vast and glorious universe emanate from the highest echelon of love. You rode in on the love vibration and you will leave on the love vibration, dear ones. The only difference between Heaven and Earth is the awareness of this fact. Once you, as physical humans, are aware of your true potential as love, Heaven on Earth shall be realized.

In creating the Earth state of being, you simply drew from your higher vibration of love and projected yourself outward, in a sense, to a state of lower vibrations. This state, in the beginning, was devoid of all light and love, meaning devoid of all awareness of love, or in presumed darkness. Why would you do such a thing? Precisely for this reason: You are creators of thought, and in order to expand upon thought, you deliberately formed a world of contrast or illusion to participate within so you might stimulate yourself toward further thought, thereby adding unto the whole of creation.

As you participate within the earthly world of illusion, you rub up against contrasts, the exact opposites of Truth, which offers you the opportunity to create new worlds. So, "As above, so below" can be said to be as much prophecy as current reality, for although the Earth was indeed fashioned in the likeness of the higher realms, its vibrational frequency is denser, a mere reflection of its heavenly counterpart. But your mission is to raise the vibrations of the Earth to match those of the higher realms, and once accomplished, you will merely move on to tackle new challenges, if you so desire. Therefore, it can be said that "as above, so below" means to imply more on the basis of "as it is above, so it will be below." Remember, dear ones, your entire goal has always been and always will be Heaven on Earth.

We would also like to remind you that you have never been alone on this journey, for you are forever anchored to and never disconnected from All-That-Is, the Source of all creation. Earth is merely a spin-off, a holographic reflection of reality, and as you work to dispel illusion upon your plane, you are simultaneously allowing Truth to appear. Although your work here is of great importance, it need not be taken seriously, for life is about spontaneity, playfulness, joy, and growth, and you are here by the sheer power of your free will. Do not forget this fundamental truth as you go about your days, for it is only through joy that the realization of Heaven shall be made known to you. Lighten up and rejoice in the fact that Earth is a reflection of Heaven, of God, and as you become aware of this fact, you shall find yourself soaring through the heavens with nary an illusion on your mind. Wake up and begin enjoying your time here. Savor the sweetness of the creative process of turning fiction into fact. From our side of the veil, we see it as the most joyous of opportunities, to be one who walks amongst the shadows of forgetfulness in order to launch a new aspect of the heavenly realms. Your intentions are good and your goals are just around the corner, so to speak. Therefore, we would encourage you to remain close to your heart, to hear its whisperings so that Heaven may become your reality all the sooner.

The Bible refers to God sending plagues to the people of Earth, depicting his wrath and eternal damnation for nonbelievers. This contradicts all I've learned about a loving God. Why was it put this way?

There are many in your world who continue to believe in the literal wording of the Bible and that is okay, for it offers a path which will eventually lead to Truth. But you must keep in mind that the Bible was written by human hands and is therefore filled with misconceptions which stem from the ego's need to create fear. Fear is the building block upon which the ego was created. It is the grandest of illusions upon the Earth plane. However, it need not be this way. To glean full understanding from the messages contained in the words of the Bible, you must rise above the ego state of mind and listen instead to what your heart is telling you. Your heart will tell you that fear is an uncomfortable place to be and should therefore be avoided. (We refer to fear as a "place," for aren't all states of consciousness referred to as "places" by the ego mind?) Fear in actuality, is merely another state of consciousness, albeit an illusory one which was created by the deceptive ego-mind. Since the ego is an illusion so too then is fear, for it is a creation of the ego, you see.

Many Biblical passages, which were written in large part by the ego, can then be said to be a fabrication of the delusional belief in fear. We are not attempting to negate the messages contained in the Bible, for they are, at their cores, of Truth, but we would encourage you to look beyond the parts that were written by the ego——those which speak of eternal damnation and plagues cast by God——and see to the core of the message, which is always that of Truth. We cannot undo that which has already been done to the peoples of the Earth. We can, however, through our words, paint clearer pictures of the messages in the Bible, thus enabling *you* to undo the messes created by the egos of your world. Far be it for us to interfere with the workings of free will. Only you, dear souls, have the ability to choose a new direction for yourself.

Realize that you have always had the choice to free yourself from the bonds of illusion, which say to you that fear exists. We say to you that no thing in the universe is evil; evil only stems from your misperceptions about seeing things as separate from yourself, which then results in the inability to see the goodness (Godness) within all things. God is all there is and you are an aspect of God. So does it make sense that God would send plagues upon Himself? No dear souls, this is merely fear speaking to you from its cowardly corner amidst the ego-mind. Release all notions that fear is real and that God punishes those who go against His wishes. The only punishment one receives is that which one brings upon oneself. You punish yourself, dear ones, and this need not be. This is the crux of our message: We hope to enable the peoples of the Earth to rise above the ego state of consciousness so you may see that what it tells you is not true. The ego is full of lies and misrepresentations of Truth, for that is what the ego is: a distorter of Truth. It acts as a filter of sorts, which, when allowed its current position at the forefront of consciousness, takes all information and filters it through the subconscious mind, thus producing fear to the conscious mind. Awaken now, children, and realize that this need not be. Allow your heart to take precedence and your current state of turmoil shall be lifted from your consciousness. Fear is an illusion, as are all things which speak to you of fear, including certain parables from the Bible. Allow it to be no more. Order the ego to take a back seat, so to speak. You shall then know that God consists of nothing but pure love energy and is therefore incapable of producing anything but Itself.

You cannot squeeze carrot juice from an orange, dear ones, and you cannot squeeze hatred or evil from love. Allow this thought to sink deeply into your being and you shall become as light as a feather, floating endlessly toward your rightful state of being. Fear and hatred are not part of your true makeup. See this as Truth and allow yourself the freedom to expand your consciousness to a state above and beyond that of ego. Pain exists only within the state of ego, and it is not a place you want to be. Make the choice now to move beyond the state in which fear exists and you shall find yourself free from illusion and in a state of eternal bliss. So be it.

Is what we refer to as the devil, Satan, or Lucifer meant to represent the ego?

You are correct in assuming as such, for the devil, Satan, and Lucifer are merely metaphors used to describe something which has no name and no face. Humanity has always felt the need to clothe all aspects of self with separate identities, and this habit has caused a great deal of confusion. However, within your hearts lie all the answers that will dispel the confusion. Oh, if you dear souls could but see the wisdom which surrounds your being, enveloped in your heart energies, you would never again feel as if the mysteries of the universe are beyond your reach. In Truth, there are no mysteries, for each of you has unlimited access to the universal bank of knowledge. Learn of your true nature and the illusion of evil, and all things associated with it shall be no more. The ego has concocted many false beliefs, such as that of separateness, lack, and evil. Realize that evil in whatever form is not real, and Satan is a concoction of the dualistic ego-mind, which is itself unreal. All things are one, part of a continual, life-sustaining Whole, and the potential for evil exists only as long as the belief in a lack of love persists. It is now time to put a stop to your belief in separation thereby allowing your True Self to reign.

Awaken now and bring yourself and your planet Home. Disavow all notions that Satan is real; Satan is only as real as you allow the ego to be. Rise above the ego and the Earth shall miraculously find itself in a state of peace and harmony, a state of love and joy, which is your rightful state. You are merely denying yourself your birthright by allowing the ego to exist. Reclaim your Divinity, children of the Earth, and we shall all be joined together in Heaven for eternity.

Is any one religion closest to the Truth?

As you're well aware, there are many religions upon your planet, each with its own set of beliefs and rules, but of one thing you can be certain: They each sprang from Truth. It is because of the egos of your world that the truth has become distorted, thereby causing much confusion and many falsehoods. These falsehoods have been allowed to seep into various religious sects in such a way that the change was barely noticeable. For this reason, many people have followed their so-called religious leaders, rather than their own internal guidance. It is tremendously important that you now begin to awaken to the Truth and realize the power you each wield. *You* are the Way, the Truth, and the Light—not some establishment.

Our point is this: At the core of any religion is Truth. However, you must first wade through the sludge of ego jargon before you can find that Truth. For this reason, we urge you to follow your own heart, rather than relinquishing your power to an establishment. Learn to go within, rather than continuing to search outside yourself for the answers you seek. The need is great at this time for each of you to begin reclaiming your personal power in order to heal the Earth of its ego-related woes. It is up to you, for only you have the power to make these changes.

Now, is there one religion more correct in its teachings of Truth? We can only say that all religions serve a purpose and within each congregation you will find those who need to be there for their own spiritual growth. Only you can decide where you need to be at any given time; therefore, we want to make it clear that we are not negating the importance of combined spirituality. Rather, we are trying to assist you in recognizing your own powers so you may derive the full benefits of whatever religion you choose. Each religion offers opportunities for growth, and amidst that opportunity is always a path which leads Homeward. Do not allow the ego to fool you into believing your religion is the only way to Truth. Many paths lead Home, and no single path is the right one for all; therefore, no single religion is the "right" path. You need only listen to your heart to stay on the path that has been laid out for you by your Higher-Self (God). It can thus be said that no one religion constitutes "better-ment" over others——merely differing opinions for those at various stages of evolution. And, we might add, there is plenty of room for all of you amidst this vast and glorious universe.

The most important thing we can say (regarding the teachings of a particular church), is to know that your power comes not from the church itself, but rather from within you, each of you. We would urge you to allow all teachings to first be filtered through your heart so they may then be presented as Truth to your conscious mind. Your heart has the capacity to take only the parts that are of Truth and discard the untruths, like water filtration systems work—they give you clean, pure water after filtering out contaminants. Your heart is not merely a muscle that pumps blood throughout your body; it is also the seat of your intuition, which allows you the power of discernment. Therefore, go to your churches, join your organized religious sects, but be forever mindful of the role your heart plays in all your earthly ventures. Only your heart can lead you Home. Therefore we would encourage you to remain close to it at all times, clutching it tightly as if it were a precious stone. For, in Truth, no stone is worth the riches of the heart. Use it wisely and it shall serve you well.

CHAPTER FIVE

Science and Modern Medicine: Pathways to Truth

"You are energy, and energy does not die; it merely recycles itself into something more interesting."

The Apostles

Is Science a Friend or a Foe to the Truth?

Firstly, all things in this grand universe, including your planet, are, in their true essence, of Truth, for Truth is all there is. When asking us if science is friend or foe, we say it can only be labeled as "friend," for the simple fact that all things spring from Truth. You see, you are each here for one reason and one reason only: To bring the light of Truth to the Earth-plane of existence. Although you may oftentimes appear to be unaware of your true purpose, in your true state (that of Soul or Higher-Self), you are always aware of your greater purpose, and all roads lead Homeward. This of course includes those participating within your scientific communities. Therefore, all knowledge which is brought forth to your planet serves to enhance the growth of the Whole, and it can thus be said that science has always been an ally to Truth. It may appear that science and religion (or spirituality) are as different as night and day, but that is all changing, for as the collective consciousness of your planet rises to meet Truth, there shall be a fusion, of sorts, an integration between the aforementioned communities which will serve to reunite that which has always in actuality been one.

You can see signs of these changes all around you. Notice how the scientific world is raising many questions and offering many answers pertaining to the nature of reality. Quantum physics will be the segment of your scientific community which will fuse Truth with physical reality in a way which will alter the appearance of science forevermore. Thus, quantum physics can be said to be the saving grace for your planet, for out of this segment of science will come the answers mankind has been seeking for many millennia. These are wondrous times indeed here on planet Earth, and all that which we've spoken about will occur in this generation. Therefore, most of you will have the opportunity to experience firsthand the changes in awareness that humanity is currently undergoing.

We would encourage you to look to science as merely another conduit through which Truth makes its entrance upon your planet. But we must point out that you need not look to science to validate the knowing each of you holds within your very own being. Each of you is a conduit for the light of Truth, and the sooner you realize this, the sooner there will no longer be a need for scientific validation of that which you already know intuitively.

One other point we wish to address here is that in reality, there is no such thing as "foe," for all things are of Truth and everything fits neatly together as pieces of a puzzle within the reality called Earth. Contrast, dear ones, is the impetus behind all growth, for without it there would be stagnation, and stagnation is not inherent in your nature. You are constantly seeking new ways to expand your knowledge, and Earth just happens to be one of the many. Look to your sciences with admiration and respect, but realize, too, that within you lies access to the same knowledge that science is now bringing forth. Look no farther than your own heart for verification of all you seek and your road Home shall be paved with gold in the form of knowledge.

What is the field of pure potentiality?

Recently, science has done much to offer a clearer picture of the true working order of the universe. Your scientists have become aware of the field of pure potentiality, but they remain unsure about the exact nature of this field. We will try to explain by saying that the universe itself is a broad, ever-expanding field of creativity. This means, simply, that all things that have ever been thought are available in this field, as well as all things that ever shall be. In other words, the universe contains all the matter needed to bring into fruition any creation which may be projected by any aspect of the Universal Mind.

You are each powerful, creative beings with the capacity to create anything your hearts desire, and the field of pure potentiality can be likened to your workshop. You are capable of "stepping" into this workshop any time you wish to do so and pull forth all the tools you need in order to create a thing from thought. Your only requirement whilst existing in human form is to learn of your true nature, which consists of your unlimited access to the field of pure potentiality. If, for example, you were to enter a garage where car engines are rebuilt, you would see about you all the tools necessary to rebuild those engines. The mechanics would have each and every tool needed for them to perform their jobs at their disposal, or the engines would not get rebuilt.

Now, imagine what would happen if the necessary tools were not available. The job would not get done, you say? Quite the contrary, for if one were to find himself in need of a certain tool, he would merely dip into the field of pure potentiality and create it, you see. You do this every day by bringing new inventions and technologies into your lives which serve to make living easier. All things that have ever been invented have come from this field of pure potentiality. For instance, when Edison invented the light bulb, he merely tapped into this vast store of knowledge and brought forth the physical manifestation of this greater knowing. All things begin as thought, and each thought originates within the field of pure potentiality.

Perhaps this issue can be clarified by referring to the field of pure potentiality as the field of all possibility, for in Truth, all things are possible. You need only think a thing and it shall be. Do you see what powerful creators you are? Look about you and realize that all things which exist within your current reality have come from pure thought. The chair in which you sit as you read these words emerged from thought, just as did the house in which you live and the space shuttles which fly your astronauts into space. From the smallest jelly bean to the most magnificent structures upon your planet, each began in the realm of thought, the field of pure potentiality. As you go about your days here on the Earth plane, you are constantly tapping into this field without your awareness of it. You need not understand the laws of the universe in order to utilize them. With your thoughts, you are creating all your life experiences each and every second of each and every day.

These thoughts originate, without exception, within the field of pure potentiality. It is as easy for you to create a jelly bean as a space shuttle. We would, therefore, urge you to begin utilizing your access to the field of pure potentiality in order to create for yourself the things you really want in your life by recognizing that it is *you* who creates your entire experience. We must point out that when we say all things originate from thought, it does not matter from whose thought, for in actuality we are all one. There is only one Universal Mind; therefore, an invention cannot be personalized, as your ego would have you believe. Rather, when you think of Edison and his great invention, and the ego says to you it's too bad you're not as wise as he to have invented the light bulb yourself, realize that in the truest sense, you did invent the light bulb. In reality, you cannot be separated from Edison, for you are each a part of the same Whole, the same Mind. Recognize that all things within your reality were created by you and start taking credit where credit is due. We might also add that each time you use a light bulb, you are reinventing it with your own thoughts by tapping into the source from which it originated.

You are each an aspect of the almighty, creative force of the universe and you each have equal access to the field of pure potentiality. There is not an exception to this rule. Know that you can have, or be, or do anything you can visualize. It is that simple, and you do it everyday; you're just unaware of it. You have become such powerful creators that it's like second nature to you, you see. Your only requirement in this lifetime is to learn to harness these powers in a way which will enable you to create for yourself only the things you want in life, rather than the things you do not want. Surely we can all agree that the things you do want consist of love and harmony, for this is all that exists within the higher realms of pure bliss, of Heaven. Begin putting your thoughts into right order and you shall soon begin to see your days filled with happiness and joy, rather than pain and disharmony. Mold the field of pure potentiality into an experience of your liking and you shall find yourself that much closer to Home.

Explain the mind/body connection.

The mind and the body are much more than just connected: they are one and the same. All that which you perceive in your world of form is nothing more than the out-picturing, the external imaging of the perceiver. The perceiver, of course, is you, each of you, and your perceptions are the result of your own thoughts. In other words, nothing can exist in your world without you to perceive it. This is precisely the notion Einstein had with his theory of relativity——all things perceived are relative to the perceiver. Your body and mind cannot exist unless you have willed them to be through your thoughts. From your true state of being, you have created your physical likeness in order to encompass your spirit, the energy essence which is the real "you." You have chosen to don a physical body to partake in various physical events that will bring you closer to the truth of Oneness. You are a spiritual entity temporarily encased in a physical body, yearning to awaken fully to the wonders of Truth. In the long run, the forgetting of Truth, of knowing who you truly are, merely serves to enhance your appreciation for the way things really are. Therefore it can be said that through your human experiences you are simply taking note, if you will, in order to better understand and thereby expand your true state of consciousness. You have merely entered a world of great contrast which offers you the perfect opportunity to expand your awareness beyond that which it has ever been.

The seeming duality of all things in your world is merely a tool to enhance the contrast of which we've just spoken. Firstly, your body gives you the impression that you are disconnected from those around you whilst you play out certain roles within the Earth life drama. And your mind is that part of your being which commands your body. Without one, you could not have the other, for in actuality they are one entity seemingly divided into separate parts. In other words, they are different aspects of the same consciousness focused upon different jobs, so to speak.

The mind is capable of healing the body because it is the body. A good analogy would be the relationship between the computer and its chips. The chips enable the computer to function. In the same way, your body is your mind's computer, as it is constantly carrying out the commands sent to it via the mind (chips).

If, for example, the mind says, "I just know I'm going to get cancer because my mother did," then your body begins responding to this order. The mind is responsible for all disease, for without the "chips" the body is capable of nothing on its own. Without the mind to believe you have a body, the body would simply cease to be. You could not take a step across a room, wipe the sweat from your brow, or feed your body the food it requires without the mind to tell you to do so.

So, the mind produces disease, but it also *heals* disease. If the body becomes overloaded with too many commands, this deluge of information produces anxiety or stress. The next time you watch the evening news, notice the numerous stories regarding statistical information pertaining to cancers and the like, and you'll notice the constant stream of worry and fear placed upon your mind by this plethora of information. When your mind repeatedly hears that you have a one-in-five chance of contracting a particular disease, it begins to calculate these odds within your psyche and your body then responds. Even the commercials blasted at you between news broadcasts are constantly announcing their own statistics.

Begin to see the massive amount of negativity that is daily thrust upon your minds and work to reverse the effects. Perhaps turn off the news and affirm: *I am healthy and whole.* Your body cannot help but respond, for that is its job. Listen to your heart, allowing it to offer peace to your mind, which will in turn produce a healthy body. Be aware of the thoughts you allow into your mind and you shall become acutely aware of the fact that it is you, your own mind, which is producing your physical body. If you desire a healthy, whole body, merely make it so by utilizing the power of your thoughts. Do not allow the ego portion of your mind to interfere with your attainment of perfection. You are perfect, dear ones, and you need only recognize this fact in order to create a perfect, whole body for yourself. In other words, as you become more aware of the truth regarding your true state of perfection, then perfect physical health will be the natural byproduct of your higher state of consciousness. The mind is an instrument, your key to creation, to be used as you see fit. We urge you, however, to create for yourself only that which will enable you to live out your days upon the Earth in peace, love, and harmony. That is the goal, and the sooner you realize it, the sooner all can return Home. Use your mind wisely and your body shall serve you well.

What is the difference between the mind and the brain?

First, the mind is all there is, for nothing exists outside Mind, hence the name Universal Mind. Who you perceive yourself to be is merely a portion, a single expression of the one Mind. If you were to picture the energy which flows through your home, lighting all your fixtures and giving power to all your appliances, it might seem as if that energy comes from different sources, but this is not the case. You know this energy flows from one source—usually an electric utility company—and by flipping a switch, you are focusing a portion of that source energy into a particular fixture or appliance. Each of you in physical form can be likened to the fixture or appliance yourself, for you are merely focusing energy into the expression of a particular personality, and God is the name you've given to the main source of supply. The God Source, we might add, is never-ending and abundant; there are no power outages in reality.

Mind is merely another name given to the all-encompassing Source which many call God. The human brain is the physical equivalent of your "portion" of the One Mind, which you are utilizing in order to focus within your present personality. Individuality, however, is a facade, an illusion, and Oneness is the only truth. Never has there been a moment when you were truly separated from the Source––you have simply entered into an agreement of sorts, which says that you would believe for a while in the illusion of separateness in order to expand thought to a point it has never before gone.

Some of you might be saying "But that still doesn't answer the original question regarding the mind and brain." We will try to explain: The world in which you now live, or are focused in, is a physical world. All that which you perceive in your physical reality is merely the physical equivalent of some aspect of Truth. This, dear souls, is the beauty of the physical universe, for you are able to take thought, which itself exists amidst the nonphysical realm, and manifest the products of your thoughts into your physical time and space to behold and enjoy. The process of creating physical reality with nonphysical thought can be quite exhilarating indeed once you understand your purpose for being here.

As we've said before, you cannot separate the thought from the thinker of the thought. The one thinker of all thought is the One Mind, of which each of you is a part. The brain is merely the physical vehicle or vessel which enables you to utilize your portion of the One Mind within physical reality. It is also a sort of calculating device which measures your position as a species within the evolutionary process upon your planet. In other words, as you collectively learn to utilize more and more of your brain power, you are simultaneously utilizing more and more of the One Mind. As you bring forth new technologies upon your plane, you are merely tapping into the knowledge of the Universal Mind. This is the process of evolution, and as you bring more knowledge regarding your true nature to the Earth plane, you are slowly but surely bringing Heaven to Earth. By this, we mean that you are bringing all the peace, love, and knowledge of Heaven––the God-state of consciousness––to the Earth plane, which will serve to raise the consciousness of humanity to the point where only peace, love, and knowledge of Truth abound. This is a great challenge for you and it serves you well for as you go about this process, you are at the same time learning much about your true nature. This Heaven on Earth state of all-knowing has been called many things, such as The Promised Land, Kingdom Come, Eden, Shangri-la, Nirvana, The New Heaven and Earth, and this is okay, for it does not matter what you call it. In Truth, it all means the same thing: evolution. Evolution is the backbone of the plan for perfection which you designed and are now implementing by participating within the earth plane of existence.

To summarize the characteristics of the mind and the brain, we would say the mind is the core of the universe. There is only one Mind, and this One Mind sustains, or gives life to all things in existence, just as your electric utility company supplies power to all your appliances. Each of you is merely utilizing a portion of the One Mind to focus within physical reality. In other words, you are expressions of the One Mind, or God, perceiving yourself as your current personality in order to carry out the evolutionary process upon the Earth plane of illusion. The brain is the vehicle which allows you to utilize a portion of the One Mind and express yourself as an individual. Your science has made you aware that the brain is stimulated by electrical impulses or wavelengths, and this means that all things within the entire universe are products of the One Mind and are made of pure energy. And as you access this energy source, you are creating your own reality. You each exist as a spark of consciousness in the Mind of God. Know that at no time are you separate from the Source, for the Source is all there is. To be separate from it would mean that you would not *be* and you need only look about you to know that you are, and you will continue to be forever. You do not go anywhere, dear ones; you merely change your point of focus from one thing to another in order to become one life form or another. Energy does not die; it merely recycles into something more interesting. And that more interesting, glorious "something" constitutes each of you in human form. There is no end or limit to what you can become, and you have an eternity to explore the vast workings of the Universal Mind. You are each loved beyond your wildest imagination, and you are held in high esteem by those of us on the other side of the veil for your willingness to participate within, thus expanding upon the true nature of All-That-Is. Once humankind is capable of seeing itself with the same degree of admiration and self-worth, you shall collectively rise to the Heaven state of awareness, returning to the point from which you originated, but with greater understanding of it.

What are your views about plastic surgery when it's used to alter one's physical appearance?

Our answer, simply stated, is that whatever changes you may desire of your physical body, it is yours to do with as you please. However, problems arise when one makes choices of this nature for reasons that exist outside of self, such as that of pleasing others. You need only be concerned with pleasing yourself. You take yourself with you no matter where you go or how you may look while you get there.

In other words, if you are altering your physical body with the intention of changing the way others perceive you, never will this be the case. It is only when your internal state, your thoughts, have changed that your experience will be altered. If, on the other hand, cosmetic surgery serves to enhance the way your feel about yourself, then we say it can be a very good thing.

All things within your physical experience or anywhere in the universe are fashioned from thought. Each new thought creates new technology, new inventions; and you are merely reaping the benefits of evolution by utilizing these innovations. As humankind learns to tap into the Source of all knowledge, your medical wonders become realities. As more and more thought is brought forth into physical manifestation, you are adding unto the growth of All-That-Is, including space shuttles, light bulbs, organ transplants, and cosmetic surgery——all that which you perceive about you. You oftentimes marvel at the great leaps your sciences are taking in advanced technology, because you are learning, as a species, to utilize your great powers. So, as you contemplate the "rightness" or "wrongness" of utilizing these technologies to your own benefit, realize that all these things have been brought into your experience to be used as you see fit. The greatest learning comes not only from using these technologies, but in their use to enhance your awareness of your true nature. You cannot change a thing about your life experience unless you first change your mind, and that is the key. Use the greater knowledge of your Higher Self, which comes to you in the form of intuition, to assist you in making the right choices and you shall never go wrong.

We would encourage you to use the technologies available to you, for in the long run, they serve to enhance the memory of who you truly are. You are perfect, whole beings, and physicality merely serves as a means for recognizing this fact. The limitations offered by the physical body afford you the perfect contrast with which to recognize your True-Self. Through evolution, humankind will eventually expand its knowing to the point where you shall be able to live upon the Earth plane amidst a state of higher consciousness, which means you will be capable of projecting your desire for a perfect physical body into your life experience without the aid of surgery. But for now, cosmetic surgery serves as a steppingstone, so to speak, toward the aforementioned goal. You are in the process of learning to become as Christs. In other words, the Christ consciousness is a state of being which allows you to traverse whatever plane of existence you wish, be it Earth or elsewhere, with a greater knowing of who you are and an expanded awareness of your creative abilities. You shall therefore be capable of expressing this knowledge through your physical body. There shall then be no more need for cosmetic or other surgery, for you will be able to produce the perfect body simply by willing it to be so. And, we might add, you already possess this capacity, but many of you have not yet tapped this source of knowledge and are therefore merely following the path of evolution toward the desired goal. However, some of you have already figured this out and are here as examples for others. Jesus was an example of this "future man." He was the perfect example of your capabilities once you've become consciously aware of the powers within you.

So, to summarize, we would urge each of you to put no more emphasis on your physical body than you would place on a cardboard box in which you have received a gift. The true prize lies inside the box. Your body is not "you"; it is merely a disposable outer casing which will eventually be discarded when its usefulness has ended. As we discuss the issue at hand, it's important that you understand the true nature of the physical body, which is that of a vehicle, not a temple. (Although we refer to the physical body as a mere vehicle, nonetheless it should be regarded with gratitude and respect for the role it plays in your physical life experience.) However, as we've said, it is yours to do with as you please, and we would encourage any activity which serves to enhance your overall life experience, for your time here is to be enjoyed, dear ones. Recognize that you have chosen your particular body for a reason, which usually entails the lesson of self-love, regardless of outer appearances. Begin to recognize the spark of Divinity that you are, no matter what the appearance of the container, and all concerns with outer appearances shall simply vanish into the nothingness from whence they came. So be it. We see you as that of absolute perfection, and once you begin to agree with us, you will find yourself that much closer to Home.

CHAPTER SIX

Creating Prosperity

"The key to good fortune lies not in the work you do, but rather in the thoughts you think."

"Doubt attached to a dream is like sandbags attached to the wings of a butterfly."

"Wishful thinking is artful creating."

"Failure is merely the seed of intent which has failed to be nourished with belief."

The Apostles

What Exactly Is Money, and Is It Okay to Have It?

Money is the energy flow of prosperity upon your planet, and since you live in a physical world, you have created the physical equivalent of the God-energy in all its various forms. God is the source of all things—including abundance and prosperity—and money is simply your means of expressing and sharing this energy with one another. It is not only okay to have money or to desire it, but money, in its truest form, is who you are. By deeming yourself worthy of having it, you are simply reclaiming a portion of your True-Self. There has been much speculation in your world regarding money as the root of all evil and so forth, which has arisen from the ego's need to see all things as separate from itself. Knowledge, joy, and abundance in all forms, including prosperity, are your inherited right, and the sooner you realize this truth, the sooner you shall return Home.

Money is not evil; no *thing* is evil. Only the delusional belief in your unworthiness has created your current love-hate relationship with prosperity. Accept now, at this instant, that all things of the universe, including money, are yours. In other words, you already own the entire universe, and to reap the benefits, you need only *allow* by deeming yourself worthy. The ego would have you believe just the opposite, and you therefore feel as if you have to work, work, work and sweat, sweat, sweat to earn a dollar or two. But we say to you there is no sweat involved in allowing the riches of the universe to flow into your experience. And you accomplish this simply by learning to love yourself. When you truly love yourself, nothing can be kept from you, for you are then able to recognize your self-worth and the important role you play in the grand scheme of things. The entire universe and all the riches within it are yours, for now and forever. In fact, they are within you, for you *are* the universe—you *are* God. Accept your right to the abundance which flows to you as easily as the air you breathe and it shall quickly manifest itself outward into the physical equivalent. This will enable you to create your own little piece of Heaven right here on Earth, which is precisely the goal.

Awaken now, children, and claim your inherited right to the abundance that you are and dollars will begin to flow rapidly into your experience. And, we might add, they will flow so rapidly that you will no longer have time for the ego's "non-sense," for you will be busy spreading your knowledge of Truth to the world, while enjoying your freedom to be, and do, and have all your heart's desires. By pronouncing yourself worthy of abundance and prosperity, you shall have added unto the growth of the whole by leaps and bounds; it is the single most important thing you can do during your present incarnation. Be free to spend, spend, spend and enjoy, enjoy, enjoy, knowing full well that the universe will supply you with the exact equivalent of your deemed worthiness. No one but you decides your worthiness. Therefore, we would urge you to awaken now to the truth of who you are, which will enable you to accept all the riches of the Kingdom as your inherited right. You are the Kingdom personified, and the sooner you realize it, the sooner you shall see abundance in all its forms begin to flow smoothly into your life. This we can promise you.

Can you give me some specific guidance for creating abundance and prosperity in my life?

There is much to be learned regarding your true nature whilst occupying the human form, and this is as it should be, for that was your intent before donning physicality. You see, when all possible learning has been gleaned from the physical experience, you shall merely return to your rightful state of being, of bliss, with a more refined sense of who you are. This is the plan, and it is perfect. You are each divine aspects of God, the Source of all abundance in the universe. Therefore, does it not make sense that you not only deserve, but already own all the riches of the Kingdom?

You, through your infinite wisdom, have created the entire physical universe with the power of your thoughts. You already possess all you could possibly desire, for nothing exists outside of you; all that which you perceive is within your very being, your mind, your consciousness. Remember, dear ones, you cannot separate the perceiver from the perceived; therefore, you cannot separate yourself from your desires. All desires erupt from within, from thought, and are then brought forth into physical manifestation via the collaborative efforts of the Whole.

And, we might add, the only reason you may not be receiving what you desire is simply because you have offered interference in the form of doubt or unworthiness. So your question might be rephrased more appropriately as: Can you give me some specific guidance for overcoming this interference? Now that we've gotten to the root of the real problem concerning abundance, we shall gladly offer assistance.

Firstly, in order to release old false beliefs and allow your True-Self to emerge fully into your life, you need only be willing to release your old ways of thinking in order to make room for the new. We, as your higher realm teachers (that portion of your self which has remained behind, so to speak, to continue that link with the universal chain) are here to guide each of you toward the acceptance of all your heart's desires. The key word here is acceptance, for it is with acceptance of the truth of who you really are into your day to day life that you will begin manifesting all your heart's desires.

Now, we understand the difficulty those of you who are currently experiencing "hard times" may have understanding this, but when you experience any form of hardship, it is simply because that is the route you have chosen to take Homeward. Humans have gotten into the habit of choosing the more difficult paths, but that is okay––whatever serves the purpose of allowing you to recognize your Divinity also serves in the expansion of the Whole. Each of you possesses the key to Truth within your own heart, and the only way human beings are capable of finding this key is by first experiencing its exact opposite, which is lack. This type of "lack" thinking is the entire basis for the Earth school curriculum. Before you journeyed into physicality from your broader, all-knowing perspective, you knew you were going to experience the exact opposite of Truth so you would become clearer within your own mind as to what Truth means to you. You purposely created many illusory obstacles, or roadblocks, which would serve to greatly enhance the truth as you work to overcome them. In other words, as you work through each obstacle, realizing its fallacy, you reemerge on the other side of consciousness with a much greater degree of awareness than that which you previously possessed.

In reality, your nature consists of pure love and total abundance in every form, but somewhere along the way you've been misled by your ego into believing otherwise. But this is how it should be in order for learning to be derived from your physical life experience. Our purpose is to assist you in removing the roadblocks, to jog the memory of who you truly are to the point that humanity as a whole shall begin moving mountains, rather than continuing to take the longer way around them. There is nothing in your experience that is not within you.

Some may say, "But I did not create that mountain, it was there when I got here." And we say that while it is true the mountain was indeed there when you arrived, it is not true that you did not create it. You see, you are each marvelous, grand creators whose only purpose for being human is to remind you of this fact. As you laboriously go 'round and 'round the mountain, you become weary of so much unnecessary treading, so much so that you realize the only way to overcome your obstacles is by finding another way. Once this is realized, then off you go in search of the "better way," which always leads to Truth.

Do you see how perfectly such a world of contrast works? Only you, as individualized expressions of All-That-Is, can come to this realization of your own accord. No one can do it for you. Becoming aware means uncovering that which is within, which must be experienced firsthand in order to be validated by your individual mind. We could preach the Truth all day, but until you experience it on your own, none of you will hear our words. This is the beauty of the Earth state of illusion, for it offers you the perfect opportunity to come into your own, as they say, to find yourself using your skills as a co-creator. Once you have fully found yourself and recognized your true Divinity, you shall merge back into the Whole, leaving behind all belief in individuation. Do you see how this works? In other words, once you have fully realized your true nature, the truth of Oneness shall lovingly enfold you back into its arms. And this, dear souls, is bliss. To fully know your rightful place amidst the universe is to live forevermore with such an overwhelming degree of love for all you've created that the thought of separation or individuation shall not be a part of your reality. This state of perfect oneness, unconditional love, absolute joy and perfection is what you call God or the Heaven state of being. This is the goal for Earth, and uncovering or awakening the truth within yourself is precisely why you are here in the first place.

Now, back to your original question, which was: "How do I specifically manifest prosperity and abundance for myself?" Our answer is simply to allow the truth of who you are to shine upon your world from its home within your heart. Use the key of knowledge to open the gates of Heaven and all the riches of the Kingdom shall spill forth at your feet. There is nothing you cannot have, or be, or do if you would only accept the truth of who you are. You are each aspects of God, majestic creators of light and love, and the only reason you may not be experiencing total prosperity and abundance is because you do not believe in yourself. It is that simple. We know many of you were hoping we would offer some magical formula to follow for creating prosperity, but we must remind you that no work is involved; there is only allowing or accepting, which comes from realizing that you already possess all your heart's desires within yourself. Sit quietly and ponder these words. Allow your heart to lead you in the proper direction. We cannot lead you along your path, dear ones, we can only point the way to the path you've laid out for yourself.

When we say to you that allowing is the key to the riches you seek, take time to absorb this information into your heart, allowing it to do the discerning. Once our words are fully absorbed into your current state of mind, you shall begin experiencing abundance in all its forms as you free yourself from the prison of illusion. The truth of who you are will literally be freed from the confines of fear, hatred, envy, and negativity of any kind and shall soar with lightening speed to the higher realms of consciousness, of Heaven, with you at the helm. You are both captain and navigator of your own ship, and the sooner you realize this, the sooner you shall begin to steer clear of the obstacles of illusion and find yourself moving through mountains as if they weren't there. In reality there are no obstacles. Obstacles are merely the products of a misplaced sense of reality.

Allow the real "you" to shine forth from your heart and the seeming obstacles shall become invisible as your heart's desires manifest within your reality. Abundance is who you are, dear ones. You need only allow the real "you" its proper place at the forefront of your consciousness. Then you shall quickly have before you everything and anything you've ever dreamt of. Find yourself, children, and all your dreams shall be realized. It is that simple.

You say we create all things in our lives with our thoughts, but isn't some of what we experience attributed to our actions as well?

When attempting to explain the exact nature of your thoughts, it is quite difficult indeed in that there are no words within your vocabulary which properly depict the truth. Nonetheless, we shall continue to work with what we've got. We would also like to point out that you each have all the knowledge of the universe stored within your heart energies, and it is our hope that through our words we will stir up these energies and unlock the floodgates to the memory of who you are. Your inner knowing, your Higher-Self, whatever you wish to call it, speaks to you not in words, but in symbols. Therefore, this form of communication is not limited, as we are here with words. Know that you are capable of much greater understanding by using your own guidance system and listening to your heart than by merely reading our words. Do not follow us, dear ones, for our purpose is not to gather a following, but rather to awaken you to the point that you need not rely on anyone other than yourself.

Now, to answer your question to the best of our ability: It is true that you are the sum total of your thoughts. You are what you think, and you create your entire life strictly by the nature of the thoughts rambling through your mind at any given moment. Some of you may be saying "But that is not true, for I have an awful disease and I know I would not have created this for myself." While we understand that you do not create these things knowingly, you nevertheless draw disease to yourself by the nature of your thoughts. And this, dear souls, is the way you get anything. You must begin to realize that thoughts are things, and each thought you project *always*—not just sometimes—manifests somewhere in the universe. Once you begin to realize this, you shall be in a much better position to create a more joyful life experience here on Earth, which was your intention in the first place.

Picture your thoughts as magnetic. See your head as a giant magnet and all thoughts spilling forth from it as magnetic waves, probing the universe to see what they can draw unto themselves. Like attracts like. If your thoughts are of a negative nature, then that is exactly what you will draw into your experience; i.e., other negative thoughts or impulses, for that is how the universe works. It is what we call law, meaning that it is absolute or unchanging. Likewise, when you consciously shift your thoughts to that of a more positive nature, then positive experiences are what you shall attract to yourself. You pull all the strings, dear ones, and it is entirely up to you which way you create: negatively or positively.

Understand also that the universe does not hear words, it merely notes your vibration. So if you are thinking negative thoughts, it does not matter so much what you are thinking, for by law you will attract all other thoughts which are of like vibration, you see. This explains how you are able to attract to yourself a certain disease you may not have known existed. Do you see how this works? Change your thoughts, change your vibration. The moment you change the vibrations you are offering the universe is the moment you change your life experience. Many of you do not understand that when you become ill, you are doing it to yourself. That is why you are here, dear ones, to learn of this truth, and we are here simply to remind you of this. Life need not be difficult in order to learn a lesson. In fact, it was your intention to enjoy your life experience when you donned physicality in order to learn more about the nature of the universe and your True Selves.

Now, how much action needs to be rendered in order to reap what you've sown with your thoughts? Very little, for thought constitutes the greater portion of what you are experiencing in your life and action need only be taken to compensate for your misuse of thought. In other words, many of you believe that by taking some form of action, you can reverse the messes you've created for yourselves. While this sometimes can be the case, it is oftentimes fruitless. Our point is that there is a much simpler way.

Again, due to the density of the Earth plane, a thought has to trudge through time before it becomes manifest within your physical reality. Since you are action-oriented peoples, you believe you need to work, work, work, and sweat, sweat, sweat to justify the fruits reaped from your labors. We say this is simply not so. You need not work for anything, dear ones. You need only allow that which is already yours into your experience by accepting the fact that you deserve it. The ego tells you that you are not deserving and you therefore believe that to have anything, you must earn it. Everything you could ever want or desire is already yours—but you've refused to accept it because somewhere along the way you've deemed yourself unworthy. This, dear friends, is the perfect example of negative attraction, for once you offered the negative thought of "I'm not worthy," your vibrations began to change, thereby altering your point of attraction. And these changes in your vibration multiplied until eventually you found yourself in utter dismay and darkness, dwelling amidst the Earth plane in a state of confusion. You are in this condition simply because you have willed it by the nature of your thoughts. Once you begin collectively to raise the vibrational level of your thoughts, thereby changing their nature, you will raise the vibrations of the Earth itself, and before long you will find yourself dwelling amidst a state of higher awareness.

But the sooner you individually make the decision to allow yourself the abundance, the prosperity, and the overflowing peace and harmony you so rightfully deserve, the sooner you shall all return Home to the heaven-state of consciousness. You need only change the nature of your thoughts by making sure they are of a positive vibration to attract unto yourself positive experiences. Remember, the universe does not hear words; it merely responds to your vibration, be it positive or negative. Simply allow yourself the pleasure of feeling good in all that you do and that will be enough to attract into your life only those things you want some of. You might be thinking: "How can I attract a specific new red car into my experience if the universe does not hear my words?" We say to you that you *are* the universe, dear ones, and if a particular red car is what you desire, then that is what you will attract—if your thoughts are in harmony with it.

Jesus said that the Father knows what you want even before you speak it, for you are the Father, you see. The formula for creating all you want is simply to have the desire and get out of your own way, for it is on its way to you at that precise moment. Only by offering negative vibrations in the form of fear or doubt will you keep it at bay. We say "at bay" here, for once you've desired a thing, you have created it. If it doesn't come into your experience, this is simply because, through your negative vibrations, you are repelling it; you push it away with negative thoughts.

There you have it, dear ones. You will always, *always* attract all your heart's desires into your life, as long as you are offering the proper vibration by focusing only upon those things you want and ignoring that which you don't want. It is that simple, and mind you, no sweat is involved.

You say we attract money into our lives by offering positive thoughts, yet a person coming from a state of lack will win the lottery. How does something like this happen?

It is true that for you to experience a thing within physical reality, you must offer the universe thoughts which are in vibrational harmony with the object of your desire. There is not an exception to this rule. Therefore, when one who appears to be living amidst a state of poverty suddenly strikes it rich, it is simply because they have, on some level of their being, attracted energy in the form of money. They have allowed it to come into their experience by offering no resistance, such as feelings of doubt, fear, or unworthiness. You each have the capacity to create anything and everything you desire simply by recognizing your powers and accepting your divinity. Oftentimes those who are creating money in their lives have merely come forth to serve as an example of this truth. Never is there a time when you experience having money or any form of abundance without allowing it to be. If you were to picture yourself as both a receiving and transmitting device which is constantly beaming signals to the universe in the form of thought and then receiving that which is in vibrational harmony with your signals (an example of like attracting like), you would have a clearer picture of your true state of being. Your world is full of examples which serve to remind you of this. As you look about, begin to notice that there is never a contradiction to this truth. You can look back upon your own experiences and see that all the circumstances in which you've been enmeshed were drawn to you as a vibrational match to your very own thoughts. You create your own reality, dear ones, and you do so with each and every thought you offer to the universe. The universe always—not just sometimes—responds by delivering unto you that which is a vibrational match to your transmissions, for that is its job. You are powerful creators, and the universe is at your beck and call. No thing is random, and each time a ticket holder wins the lottery, we can assure you there is a far grander reason than just pure luck. Look to others as shining examples of your own powers and you shall quickly rise above the embers of illusion. Seek no more outside yourself, for the key to good fortune lies not in the work you do, but rather in the thoughts you think. Offer only pure, loving, prosperous thoughts and the universe has no choice but to match them with the vibrational equivalent of good fortune.

How long does it take for something to manifest in our lives?

Firstly, we must remind you that all that which you perceive in your daily lives was brought forth from the realm of thought. The road upon which you drive and the vehicles in which you travel those roads are manifestations of thought. When asking us to place an exact time frame upon the physical manifestations of thought, we can only say that it depends entirely upon the individual who creates the thought. For instance, if one desires something very much, then the emotion of great desire coupled with the thought will bring about the manifestation more quickly than would thought alone.

You each live amidst your own little world, which is seemingly separate from one another, with your own set of beliefs attached to your very being. In other words, each of you creates your own reality according to your beliefs, and no two realities are exactly identical. Therefore, you are each your own universe. You've probably heard the expressions "macrocosm" and "microcosm." We say that the microcosm you perceive yourself to be––the universe within the universe––should more aptly be interpreted to mean that you are the universe. Thus, we can eliminate the word "microcosm" altogether. See what little credit you give yourself? The truth is that you are the macrocosm, the entire universe, wrapped up neatly in a package labeled "you." And the differences you experience lie not in the universe itself, but rather in your perceptions of it. You each have a unique angle from which to view life, and your point of view is just as important as the next one, for without it the universe would not be a complete Whole. Do you see how this works? In other words, you each exist as an aspect, a piece of the Whole, whose only differences lie in which piece of the Whole you are choosing to experience. As you go about your days, observing life from your unique perspective, you are adding greatly to the knowledge of the Whole. And each thing or circumstance you create for yourself serves this same purpose. All things which manifest in your physical reality are first born of thought, and the desire that propels the thought emerges from Spirit's eagerness to project Itself into physical reality. This, dear souls, is the purpose for your humanness. This physical time and place offers you the opportunity to expand your thoughts and desires into that of a physical form. This process is quite exhilarating to your True-Self—nothing is more exquisite than bringing forth the nonphysical energy of who you are in order to create physical forms. You, dear ones, are the same stuff of which worlds are made.

The key to realizing your dreams more rapidly is to bask in the desire that originally accompanied the thought. The things that are manifested more quickly than others are those which have the impetus of great emotion behind them, you see. This process can also be applied to something you do not want, such as poverty or illness. You draw these unwanted things into your life by giving your attention to them whilst offering powerful emotions, such as fear.

When you really want something to manifest in your lives, offer the positive emotions of joy and expectation, which are the vehicles upon which your desires ride in. When you really don't want something, yet you fuel this unwanted thing with great emotion, you are drawing that which you don't want into your experience.

So, as you can see, there is no exact science to the laws of creation as they pertain to your linear time. We can only say that all things you desire manifest somewhere in the universe and begin making their way to you at once. And, the only way you do not realize a desire is if you counteract it with negative thoughts such as fear, doubt, or unworthiness. There you have it, the key to creation. We might add, it has been within you all along, but humanity has merely been looking in the wrong places for quite some time. By this, we mean that mankind has been searching all these years outside itself for that which can only be found within. Go within, dear peoples, and pluck the desires from your heart, allowing them to manifest and become part of your reality by charging them with great emotion in the form of belief (expectation), joy, love, and the acceptance of your own worthiness. Then stand back and watch the sparks fly as your majestic creative powers begin to work miracles in your life. You have only to believe in yourself in order to receive all that which you desire. Once you know where to look (within yourself), all your dreams shall begin springing forth from your heart and into your physical reality with such rapidity that it will boggle your mind. So be it, dear ones. Our hope is that you will each find within yourselves the key which will allow you to manifest all your heart's desires, thereby allowing you to live amidst a state of abundance and joy while here on the Earth plane.

This was your original intent, but you oftentimes slip into the pool of negativity, drowning your dreams along with yourself. Allow this to be no more. Awaken, children, to the truth of who you are and allow your light and love to cast out the shadows of illusion and negativity, so that you may create for your world only that which comes from God. Allow the peace, love, and harmony of the God-state, or Heaven-state, to shower down upon the Earth from its home within your heart and soon all humankind, as well as the Earth itself, shall realize the dream of Heaven on Earth. You shall have your Kingdom right here, which will enable you to enjoy the fruits of physicality amidst a state of pure bliss. And this shall be Paradise, dear ones. Whoever said you can't have your cake and eat it too?

How can I find my purpose in life?

By listening to your heart—it is that simple. Your heart energies are focused upon and centered around your higher state of being. The promptings you receive from this source come in the form of intuition. Your intuition is your greatest tool in this lifetime, for if you heed it, it will allow you to remain upon your intended path at all times. None of you have come forth into this physical lifetime without some sort of agenda. And all of you are constantly receiving guidance from your Higher Self, but many of you have allowed your intuition to become dormant, and your ego so dominant that you are unable to be aware of this guidance, let alone follow it. In other words, this continuous guidance is oftentimes ignored. And this, dear souls, is the single most common reason that many of you find yourselves in a state of confusion.

You each came forth with desires and aspirations, and you must let these desires be expressed, rather than continuing to allow your ego and society at large the power to negate your dreams. Dreams and aspirations are merely your subconscious memories, your Higher-Self's way of prompting you to do what you came here to do. If you were to go back in your life and remember what it is that you've always dreamt of doing or becoming, whether it be an actor, a writer, a doctor, an astronaut, or a parent perhaps, you will always find your purpose. You intuitively know what you came here to do; you have merely allowed your intuition to take a back seat by listening to the ego's untruths instead.

We say, listen no more to the ego's non-sense, for you can have, or be, or do all that which your heart desires, and you are here merely to realize this fact. The sooner you do so, the sooner you shall find yourself in a higher state of truth and awareness. Follow your heart, dear ones, thus allowing yourself the freedom you so desperately seek. All your hopes, dreams, and aspirations are wrapped up neatly in a package labeled "you." Once you begin to unwrap the layering––the strings of untruth and non-sense that have you so wrapped up in illusion––you shall find yourself shining the light of who you are upon your planet by becoming the embodiment of your dreams. May we suggest that you begin by seeing yourself as worthy. You are a Divine child of the universe, an aspect of God, and we cannot think of a thing more worthy than that. Trust your inner knowing and it will paint for you a beautiful portrait filled with all your heart's desires.

Then jump headfirst into this portrait of dreams, knowing full well that you will emerge on the other side with greater knowing and a much greater sense of accomplishment. The only way to "lost-ness" is to follow the ego, and the only way to truth is by following the heart. Heed these words, children, and come Home to the highest state of knowing, where the wonderful, glorious being within you belongs.

CHAPTER SEVEN

Views from a Higher Perspective

"All you need to do is find your Self and all your dreams will follow."

"To worry is to place your faith in the least desired outcome."

*"The power to think **is** the divine power of God."*

The Apostles

Sin

Sin, as with all things in your earthly world of illusion, is not real. In reality there is only that which consists of pure love energy. All else is but illusion, a false fragment of the separated ego-mind. Firstly, we would like to explain the nature of the Earth plane, so you may get a better picture of Truth. The Earth plane is the exact opposite of Truth, and this is because it serves to stimulate thought, thereby adding unto the growth of the Whole. When creating the Earth, you simply took the Truth and turned it upside down. All that which you perceive as truth upon your plane is unreal and need only be turned around, flipped to the other side of the coin, in order for Truth to be seen. As you participate in your world of illusion, it is the process of "flipping the coin" that serves to enhance your knowledge of who you truly are.

The belief in sin is merely another illusion crafted by the ego's need to see all things as opposites to Truth. Sin does not exist, and from our vantage point, we know that all that which you perceive as sinful are merely lessons along the road to enlightenment. By "enlightenment," we mean the process of becoming aware of one's true nature.

We know many of you may be asking, "But how can you say that one who takes the life of another has not committed a sin? After all, the Bible says, 'Thou shall not kill.'" Firstly, we say to you that there is no death; therefore, how can there be the sin of causing a death? Secondly, we would like to address the issue of the Ten Commandments. These commandments were set forth to offer you a format, of sorts, to follow that would lead you closer to Truth. In reality, the only one harmed by committing a presumed sin is the one doing the "sinning." Although one cannot, in reality, harm another, he can draw undesirable experiences to himself by *intending* to harm another. Do you see how it works? It's all about mind, dear ones, for your state of mind is all there is. Therefore, when referring to the Ten Commandments set forth by Moses, be aware that these words of wisdom were meant to save one from oneself, not that of another.

Again—we cannot stress this point *enough*—*you do not die*; nothing dies. You are pure energy that exists within a perpetual state of recycling. Murder is the ultimate sin on Earth, but can you not see how the sin of murder is just another ego-woven illusion which says to you, through your fears, that death exists? It simply cannot be. You are magnificent, glorious light-energy beings who exist for now and for eternity. The sooner you come to this realization, the sooner you shall stamp out the flames of fear that are spreading upon your planet. Then you will begin seeing things as they truly are. Remember, it is the process of turning illusion into Truth that serves you well in this lifetime. May we suggest that you begin turning your illusions around in order to see the other side, which is always that of Truth. It is the only way, and we know of no better place to start with than the likes of sin. Sin does not exist, death does not exist, and mistakes or misdeeds of any kind are but illusions. All that which you experience in your daily life serves to advance the awareness of the Whole.

The plan is perfect and there are no mistakes——merely Truth playing a game of hide-and-seek with the inhabitants of Earth. The greatest hint we can give you for winning the game is to remind you where to look. And that, dear ones, is always within yourself, your heart, for nothing exists outside of you. Go within and seek the Truth, and your heart shall whisper great things to your inner ear. Know that only peace, love, joy, and abundance exist within Reality, the higher state of Mind many call God or Heaven. The God state of mind waits patiently within your very being until you are ready to find It. This potential within each of you does not lie dormant; it constantly speaks to you, urging the ego-conscious part of self to rejoin the rest of self in the state of eternal bliss. Once you have found it, you shall proclaim, "This truly is Paradise." Welcome Home.

Aging

You grow old and die simply because your beliefs tell you that you will. You are constantly bombarded by the news media, who tell you that you have a one-in-five chance of contracting cancer, or that your bones will eventually deteriorate as you age due to a lack of calcium, or any number of different "factoids." If you accept these statements and internalize them, turning them into beliefs that you accept as strongly as you accept the fact that the sky is blue, they will then become parts of your experience. If, as you hear the news media reporting various statistics gathered from someone's data (which, by the way, are always a matter of opinion), you begin to notice negative emotions stirring within you, such as fear, in response to the statistics, then you are at that moment creating the conditions you fear.

Remember Job's quotation: "For the thing which I greatly feared is come upon me." You are, in essence, taking the beliefs of others and enfolding them within your own psyche, pronouncing yourself to be a statistic. If, on the other hand, you were to allow such false beliefs to go in one ear and out the other, so to speak, without offering negative emotion as a response, you would then have chosen not to become a statistic.

Unless you offer negative thoughts on the subject of disease in the form of doubts or fears, perfect health shall be your experience during this physical lifetime. In regard to aging: If you believe that you will grow old, wither, and eventually die, then that shall be your experience. Should you ask whether aging is a necessary prerequisite to earth-life, we would say that aging and death are never prerequisites to anything, for in reality, these things simply do not exist. You have absolute freedom to create anything you want for yourself. If death and the aging process are your choices of experience, then so be it. It can be quite difficult for one to reverse such strong, deeply ingrained beliefs, but it is certainly not impossible––nothing is impossible for such powerful beings as yourselves. Aging need not be part of your Earth life experience. You always have the capacity within you to alter your experience simply by altering your beliefs and keeping your attention focused only upon those things you want to experience whilst ignoring all the rest.

Poverty

One lives in poverty quite simply because he has chosen to do so. Again, you each come into this physical life with some type of agenda. By this, we mean that you have chosen this vast realm of contrast in order to experience its various attributes. If living amidst a state of poverty and seeming lack is one's chosen experience, then so be it, for you are each free to choose anything you desire. Whatever choices you make whilst occupying human forms, we can assure you they are always done with the intent to serve the Whole. "How can I best serve my brothers?" is a cry often heard from those going into human battle. We are not implying that the Earth is a hopeless war ground. Rather, we say that although the Earth may appear to be in a state of never-ending struggle, it is nonetheless in the state of becoming.

All that which you perceive around you as negatively charged, such as war, hatred, homelessness, famine, and disease, are merely rungs in the evolutionary ladder which will eventually enable the Earth plane to reach its ultimate goal of Heaven. You will have your Heaven on Earth, but you must take the steps, one by one, to get there. When you see someone living in poverty, realize that they are there by their own choice, which is always for the "better-ment" of all. Know, too, that one living in poverty is never beneath one who is not. You are each equal in every sense of the word, and you are all carrying out your chosen tasks, which serve to bring humanity closer to the truth of Oneness.

However, although a brother or sister has chosen to submerse himself or herself in an impoverished state of being, you can serve the Whole even better by offering your assistance to help bring that person out of this state. Poverty is used not only as a contrast to remind you of what you are *not*, it can also serve as a doorway into that which you *are*. The next time you see someone wallowing in the presumed pain of poverty, take them by the hand and help lead them home. With an act such as this, you shall have benefited the Whole tenfold. Oftentimes one is in a poverty state simply to offer another the chance to help.

Trust in the Divine knowledge of each soul and know that each one knows exactly what they are doing. Each and every one of you exists in human form merely to assist in bringing one another Home. Begin to see your true purpose for being as human and you shall begin to love one another, as was intended. You are mighty light warriors, serving one another out of your love for All. Know that what we speak is true and the peace that comes from the realization of this knowledge shall be the impetus which propels humanity to the gateway of the heavenly spheres.

An Eye for an Eye

If everyone were to truly live by this standard, how many of you do you think would be left standing? Therein lies your dilemma, for you cannot merely take a handful of misdeeds and wrap them up nicely to be presented as sins worthy of punishment without packaging all misdeeds within the same confines. Again, in reality, there are no sins; merely lost souls seeking themselves. Therefore, if there are no sins, how can there be punishments? The "eye for an eye" expression is nothing more than the justification of punishment for presumed sins, and this, dear souls, simply cannot be. Let us remind you of the truth of Oneness. Since all is One, can you not see how placing blame and punishment upon another is in actuality punishing yourself? Would you be willing to pluck out your own eye because you had made a mistake? You must learn, dear peoples, to reach deep within your heart and bring forth kindness and understanding to those poor souls in need, rather than adding to their pain by offering to remove an eye.

Jesus said: "Or how wilt thou say to thy brother, Let me pull out the mote out of thine eye; and, behold, a beam *is* in thine own eye?" (Matthew 7:4) This means simply that you cannot know what is taking place at the soul level of another human being under any circumstances. Therefore, you are not to judge another's actions according to your own beliefs. One might ask, "How can I not judge another when he has taken the life of my beloved?" We say to you that you cannot know what is taking place at the soul level of the "victim," just as you cannot judge the perpetrator's actions. You must trust that each soul knows exactly what it is doing. When viewed from our perspective, one sees clearly that no act, no matter how seemingly heinous, is random. Each and every act is carefully orchestrated within the play of life, and it is designed to bring about a particular healing or lesson to those involved in it.

Therefore, the next time someone steps on your toes or the toes of someone you love, look within the act to its core and see the messages of Truth being offered. We can assure you that at the core of every act is a message of Truth. It is up to you to uncover it. We would urge you to not be so quick to point fingers of blame and judgment, for there is no way possible for you to understand the reasoning behind each and every act whilst occupying the human form. You can only know what a particular act means to you, and that is all you need to be concerned with. Open your heart to the truth of Oneness and love, and the feelings associated with vengeance shall be no more. Realize that, in reality, there are no sins, and certainly no punishments. The sooner you realize this, the sooner we shall all reach the goal of bringing the Earth plane home to its highest potential state of perfection.

Homosexuality

Many who are living within the darkened parameters of the ego tend to view all things unlike themselves as evil, yet evil does not exist outside of the delusional state of ego-centered consciousness. The ego tells you that all things outside of and different from yourself are to be feared. Firstly, nothing exists outside of you, and secondly, nothing is different from you, for all things are one and the same. How can you find differences in something that is inseparable? It simply cannot be done, dear ones. Your only differences lie in your differing perspectives.

The next time the ego says to you that a loving relationship between two human beings of the same gender is blasphemous, realize that no love, in whatever form, is blasphemous, for in Truth, love is all there is. All things around you merely serve as "props" designed to enhance the awakening of the spirit in mankind. This includes other people as well as circumstances surrounding your daily lives. Learn to rise above the ego in order to see into the core of anything, which is always that of Truth. Never look upon another with contempt or hatred in your heart, for this has a way of boomeranging and striking the sender of the thought.

Your thoughts manifest as tangible things, and you must be forever mindful of their nature. Negative thoughts hold you in bondage. Positive thoughts free you to do all you are capable of doing, thereby spreading the love of who you are to all corners of the universe. Only when humans are ready to look at each other with nothing but love in their hearts will you be able to collectively rise above the ego state of consciousness and come Home. It is up to you, peoples of the Earth. The time is right for these changes to occur, and all you need to do is look about you to see that they are well under way––with you or without you––the choice is yours. "Thy will be done, in Earth as it is in Heaven." So be it.

We would urge each of you to hop aboard the expressway to Heaven. However, excess baggage in the form of hatred and contempt is not permitted. The only ticket which entitles you to a seat upon this railway is the ticket of Truth, which, by the way, you already have in your possession. All you need to do is seek it from within and it shall be handed unto you from the ticket booth within your heart; first-class seating, we might add. Do not be left dumbfounded and ticketless, dear ones, as the train pulls out. Instead, learn to love one another *because* of your seeming differences––not in spite of them. No longer allow the ego to place judgments upon another due to whom they have chosen to love. That love is chosen at all upon your planet is indeed a miracle. See this as Truth and spread your love, dear ones, thus claiming your one-way ticket Home. Remember, the express train is headed that way, with or without you. Therefore, we would urge you to pack your bags quickly by putting your thoughts into right order.

The Death Penalty

As seen from your perspective, the death penalty is very real, and it is the topic of much heated debate upon your plane. However, from our point of view, the death penalty remains strictly within the confines of the illusory ego-mind. In other words, death does not exist, nor does sin; therefore, how can one be put to death for acting in a sinful way? Do you see our dilemma here? For we surely do not wish to dispel the lessons you have created for the unfolding of your Earth-play drama, but we do wish to assist you in overcoming the non-sense that causes you pain, for this need not be.

Our intent is to help you rise above a state of pain so that you may enjoy your experiences upon the earth plane, rather than continuing to assume that to learn a lesson, you must wallow in misery.

Such beliefs say to you that you have to work hard for a thing and that nothing has been earned unless sweat is involved. No, dear souls, you are each inheritors of the universe; the Kingdom of Heaven is yours, and the sooner you come to recognize this fact, the sooner you shall come to see that you do not have to work for anything, for all things of the universe already belong to you. They were handed down unto you as your birthright by our great Father in Heaven. Therefore, when one of the Earth finds themself in the "hot seat," rather than condemning them for their actions, offer instead to take them by the hand and lead them homeward. Those who act in ways deemed unfit by your society have merely become frustrated in their attempts to find the good within themselves. If all the peoples of the Earth were to see fully who they truly are, there would be no more bloodshed, no more disease, and no more famine. From this point of clarity, can you not see how the aforementioned maladies would disappear?

War erupts because a person or a country possesses something another wants, which springs from the "lack of" thinking that says to you there is not enough of a thing to go around. Therefore, you feel as if you have to fight to stake your claim for your piece of the pie. But if you could understand and accept that the universe is abundance itself, that all things desired are in never-ending, abundant supply, then you would quickly see that there is plenty of pie for everyone. In fact, each of you is a personification of the entire pie.

Now, we would say that never is the act of deliberately intending to harm another condoned from our world, but the key word here is "intending." In Truth, one is not capable of harming another, although one may intend to do so. Do you see how this works? You can only hurt yourself by the thoughts you think and the intentions you hold. Therefore, when you recognize that no one can harm you and you certainly do not die––you merely go from life to life––then you can see that it is the criminal who is in torment, not the so-called victim.

Realize that you cannot escape yourself, so if, for example, you were wallowing in torment because of your intention to harm others, then no matter how you exit the Earth plane, whether by death from natural causes or death by execution, you will still take yourself wherever you go. Until you make the decision to change your thought patterns by allowing the goodness within you to emerge, you shall remain in torment for as long as it takes for the emergence of Truth to occur.

So, to answer your question: No, we do not condone the death penalty per se, but at the same time, we know that death does not exist, so we are merely playing along with you by answering this question. What we are saying is that we do not condone the *intent* to cause harm to another, whether or not you believe the harm is justified. Remember, it's the intent which causes the problem, and it is the thinker of the intent who bears the repercussions. Therefore, be it wise for you to step aside, allowing each soul to carry out its part amidst the drama of life and be content to carry on with your life whilst the universe takes care of the details. Center your mind only on things that are good (of God), and that shall be all you are able to perceive in your day to day life.

Darwin's Theory of Evolution

Darwin's theory of evolution is just that: a theory. It nonetheless served a purpose in that it allowed the peoples of your world to begin questioning the nature of their being more extensively. All things are given to the Earth for a reason, and they always serve to awaken the spirit of man to the truth of All-That-Is. Darwin's theory has caused a great deal of speculation, and many eyebrows were raised that otherwise would not have been. Due to this single theory, many peoples of the Earth, along with the scientific community, have expended much energy toward trying to either prove or negate this theory. Therein lies its purpose. Without this theory to ponder, many would have merely carried on with their lives, never stopping to question their existence. It has served its purpose and quite well indeed. Because of this one theory many alternate theories have sprung forth which have also served to bring the Truth to the forefront of human consciousness.

This process can be likened to the paring of an onion. To reach the core, you need to remove the outer layers, one by one, disposing of the unnecessary parts in order to reach your true destination. Darwin's theory can be said to be merely another layer of the onion, which, when proved unnecessary, can be thrown in the waste can with the other falsities. In your state of humanness, it is necessary to see the unfolding of Truth in this fashion. You need to prove to yourselves, beyond a reasonable doubt, that a thing is not useful before you are able to throw it away. Darwin's theory has brought many peoples of the Earth to a state of higher awareness. Upon registering this theory within their psyches, many of them came to the conclusion that it didn't "feel" right, and off they went in search of more viable answers.

"If man did not evolve from ape, then where did he come from?" you might ask. Our answer is that all species upon your plane evolve within their own lineage. Therefore, current man evolved from past man-consciousness, just as current ape forms evolved from past ape-consciousness. We would like to pose a question for you to ponder: If human evolved from ape, then why is the ape still known to you? Does it make sense to assume that only certain apes were able to transform themselves into human beings while the rest were left to remain entirely ape-like? Do you think, perhaps, that a few apes just got lucky while the rest were doomed to eternal ape-hood? This dear souls does not fit anywhere into your current state of reasoning. All members of a species evolve, not merely portions of it. Evolution, as you see it, and evolution in Truth do not coincide. The true meaning of evolution is spiritual growth, not physical metamorphosis. However, the advancement derived from knowledge or spiritual growth is projected outward and into the physical form.

Therefore, humankind, through knowledge gained, has been able to awaken its senses in ways which have allowed for the better usage of universal knowledge. Due to this spiritual growth, you are presently more capable of tapping into, so to speak, the Universal Mind, which is filled with all the wisdom of the universe. Hence your present-day wonders, such as computers and space travel. Primitive man, as a whole, was not able to tap into this source as readily, for he was not yet aware of its existence or availability. You have evolved from this primitive state of darkness and are now more capable of putting your thoughts to good use. You are learning to master your thoughts, thus manipulating the forces of the universe into physical form. You have come a long way, but there is still much to learn. And that is precisely why you dear souls are here, working diligently to bring yourselves and your planet to the highest state of awareness, which can be called the top rung of the evolutionary ladder.

Once you have reached this goal, there shall be much laughter and celebration within your hearts, as well as a great sense of accomplishment. Awaken now to this truth and allow your heart to sit in the driver's seat, for by allowing your heart to lead you, the realization of this goal shall be hastened tenfold.

Youth Violence

When speaking of the many atrocities the ego has created, crime in relation to children can seem to many to be the most appalling. However, as with all things, there is a purpose for this, too. If you were to stand back and view your world from a higher perspective, you would clearly see the reasoning behind such deliberate, attention getting acts. The children who seem to be destroying your planet and each other are, in actuality, on a mission to accomplish quite the opposite. Many of the souls encased in today's youth are merely putting forth effort in the hope of saving humanity from itself.

You see, dear ones, when your energies are continually expended toward the ways of ego, such as violence, hatred, racial issues, disease, and so on, it is yourselves and the Earth that suffer. Of course, all that which we've just mentioned is only another step in the ladder of spiritual evolution, but the time has come to put a halt to the ego's rampage. The violence you are currently experiencing with your children is a direct result of the ego's need to reign supreme on your planet, which means that, in large part, most of you still see yourselves as separate from the Whole, and therefore you still believe in the illusion of darkness. The peoples of the Earth have chosen, collectively, to ignore the one thing most precious to your world——your children——whilst you look outside yourselves for peace and material gain. However, these things can never be found outside of self; peace and prosperity can only be found in their home within your heart.

Many of your children have suffered due to this lack of love and affection, just as many adults continue to suffer due to the lack of understanding of who they really are. Therefore, it has been necessary for many souls to return to Earth, sounding their trumpets of despair, in order to get your attention. The youths of today are simply mirroring the nonsensical beliefs of humanity as a whole.

You are the creators of all that which manifests in your world, thus we can conclude that you have collectively created the turbulence which abounds around your young people. However, you are also quite capable of hearing the messages being brought forth through your children and thereby reverse the problem. Look to your youth with an open heart and an open mind and know what it is they are offering your world. Hear their messages loudly and clearly in order to begin cleaning up the messes your egos have made. Realize that the offenses being created by your children are merely lessons which serve to perpetuate Truth. Read between the lines of each circumstance and rescue yourselves and your youth from the dis-ease caused by the ego mind.

Wake up now, children, and come Home. Heed the cries of your offspring and open your hearts to them. Then the Earth shall begin to heal itself of all its woes. Put more emphasis on the things that truly matter, such as family, love, and participation in one another's spiritual growth. No longer remain centered in the egotistical ways of materialism. Rather, reverse the problems related to your children by reversing your way of thinking. We ask only that you allow your heart to be your guide and peace shall be yours forevermore. The violence within your inner cities shall cease as people awaken to the remembrance of who they truly are. You are grand and glorious beings of light and love, and your knowledge of this fact has merely been temporarily diluted by the ego's shadow. Awaken now and bring yourselves and your children Home to the heaven-state of consciousness, where only peace and love abound.

Intuition

When you made the decision to journey to Earth and become a physical expression of life, you wanted reassurance that although you would be limited as to what your memory could hold, you would nevertheless remain in constant contact with that higher part of yourself, which many of you refer to as Soul. You see, dear ones, there is a very grand purpose to your being human, for it aids in the growth of the Whole. This can oftentimes be difficult to see for those of you with limited vision, and therein lies the reasoning for your intuition.

Intuition is your direct link Home. It is a constant flow of energy between your physical self and your Higher Self which allows you to remain connected at all times to All-That-Is. Never are you separate from God; you only think you are. Think of your intuition as a source of energy that you are able to perceive with your physical senses, such as a beam of light. This will make it easier for you to picture the connection of which we speak. Now, envision this beam of light as stretching all the way from Heaven to each individual on Earth. In other words, picture a large ball of light as the very core of the universe and then imagine rays or beams streaming out from that one great Source in as many directions as there are human beings.

It may help to see these rays as rubber band-like, stretching to allow all the freedom you need without constricting your movements. Now, imagine that this ball of light, this main source, contains all the knowledge of the entire universe, meaning all that which has ever been thought by an aspect of All-That-Is. Next, imagine that this ball of light is full of radiant love energy, and that it is the inspiration, the breath of life, which is breathed into all things in existence. Now, see that this light does indeed exist, for it is what many of you have labeled God, and the beams of light emanating from but never separated from this source are each of you in human form.

Your rubber band-like beam of light, which you carry around with you wherever you venture into the universe, be it Earth or elsewhere, is your connection to the God Source. You may wonder what all this has to do with intuition. It is precisely this: The beam of light of which we've mentioned, and which can be seen by those of us on our side of the veil but remains elusive to those of you with limited vision, is what you have termed intuition. These beams of light shoot directly from the God Source and into your very own heart energies, which means that God is within your heart.

The God Source can then be likened to lighted energy from which we each emanate. And through your intuition, your ray of light, you are capable of accessing all the knowledge of God. All you need to do is to recognize this and thereby realize that you are "tapped into" this abundant source of knowledge at all times; many of you are just unaware of it. We might take this time to point out that names and pronouns do much to limit your view of reality. When referring to "God" or "Him," realize that, in reality, energy is all there is. Once you are able to grasp the notion that God exists not *only* in human form, but in energy form or in spiritual form, comprehension will be much easier. To be more specific, Gods exists not only in human form, for He is surely that by expressing Himself as you,

you see, but God is much more than human, for He is the energy source which animates all living things.

We hope our analogy has painted a clearer picture of intuition. However, if you are seeking more knowledge, simply go within and pluck the information directly from your own link with All-That-Is. You must understand, children, that you are privy to this vast store of knowledge any time you so desire. Therefore, we encourage you to open your hearts and "dip" into this source, and your lives shall be much easier indeed. We have just handed you the key. It is up to you, however, to put it to good use. God is not going anywhere——He shall merely wait patiently until you are ready to rejoin Him in the state of eternal bliss.

Meditation

Your conscious physical self can be likened to that of a transmitting-receiving device with which you both transmit and receive thought. However, you cannot simultaneously receive and transmit. Meditation is merely the name given to the process of quieting the transmission of thought in order to hear the reception of thought. This process can be likened to a radio station where the broadcasters are only transmitting, while those on the receiving end can only receive. You cannot use a radio to transmit information; you can only receive information. Therefore, if you picture yourself in like manner, you will see that you are clearly and continually transmitting and receiving communications to and from the universe, but you cannot do both at the same instant.

So, we encourage those of you who are contemplating doing meditation to view it as we have just described, which will allow for greater understanding and manipulation of thought. All thought, whether it comes from your conscious ego mind or the universe at large, is yours to do with as you please. Your purpose here is simply to mold thought into an object or circumstance of your liking. Thought exists as intangible, nonphysical energy which is manipulated and formed into something physical upon your physical plane. This is the entire purpose of physical dimensions such as Earth. You are merely taking something nonphysical (thought) and molding it into its physical equivalent (form). This process is quite exhilarating, is it not? And all the more so when you become aware of your purpose for being in this physical realm.

You can surely all agree with our analogy here, for you know that our description is accurate. How many of you are able to sense your thoughts with one of your five senses as they make their way through the corridors of your mind? It cannot be done, for thought itself is nonphysical energy. As you view the things in your life which have manifested from the realm of thought—which includes everything in your physical existence—you can clearly see the magnificence of your creative powers at work. In the physical realm, you are offered the opportunity to see and touch and smell the manifestations of your thoughts. Meditation is simply a means of receiving inspiration and guidance from the non-physical part of yourself (your Higher-Self), which you then add unto your own thoughts, and together you create worlds.

You see, as you go about your life here on the Earth plane, thousands of thoughts race through your mind during each moment of your waking state, and oftentimes these thoughts are inspired by the ego-mind, which works diligently to maintain your belief in illusion. But you also have just as many thoughts transmitted to you from your Higher perspective, which override the falsity of the ego's notions. You may hear such statements as, "There's got to be more to life than this, or "I know I'm more important than society tells me I am." These sorts of positive reassurances are always coming to you from your higher, inner guidance, which is forever expressing to you that all really is well, no matter what your current circumstance may be. How do you learn to differentiate between your ego and your Higher-Self?

Meditation is as good a place to start as any, for as you meditate—that is, allow yourself to receive rather than transmit—you will begin to get a sense of what the receiving of thought feels like, versus that of the ego-based transmission of thought. We might add that both the transmitting and receiving of thought feels quite similar, but there is a subtle difference that you can learn to detect quite easily through the practice of quieting your mind of transmissions. So, if you are comfortable with meditation, we would encourage it. However, realize that meditation, as with all things of your world, comes with a lot of unwarranted, preconceived notions attached to it. Meditation requires no formal training, no special clothing, and no particular position in which to sit in order to receive; you can meditate standing on your head just as effectively as you can in lotus position. For remember, the only purpose for meditation is to become aware of the guidance continually being offered to you, rather than continuing to ignore it, as is too often the case. The greater purpose for all of this is to expand your awareness so that you can live out your days on the Earth plane with complete understanding of why you are here in the first place.

Therefore, if you are pondering meditation, know that there are no rules. Do whatever you feel comfortable doing, wear whatever you want to wear, and sit in any position and in any location you choose, for these things do not matter. All that does matter is that you understand your true purpose is simply to *hear* the wise guidance continually being offered to you by your Higher-Self, so that you can utilize this guidance to create a better life for yourself. Once you've established this connection, or better yet, become aware of it (for it is always there), you shall find your life filled with more peace, love, and happiness than you've ever experienced before, simply because you will be allowing the voice of Truth to override the ego's nonsense for perhaps the first time. We can assure you it shall be well worth the effort, or, to be more precise, the *allowance*.

Unanswered Prayer

Firstly, know that your prayers are answered at all times, for there is nothing you may ask for that you do not receive; albeit, you may not always be aware of it. In the greater sense, nothing occurs in your daily life that you did not ask for on some level of your being. One may say, "But my young child was just murdered, and I certainly did not ask for that!" While we agree that in your current state of consciousness you could not possibly fathom creating such a seemingly horrific event, we will not agree that you did not create it, or better yet, agree to participate within the circumstance. Do not see us as heartless as we attempt to clarify this delicate issue. Rather, realize that we are seeing from a higher, clearer perspective which enables us to view, in truth, the happenings upon your planet.

Now, as we've previously stated, you each emerge into this physical life with some sort of an agenda, a blueprint, so to speak. The events which unfold in your lives, whether good or bad, are merely the result of this blueprint. You see, nothing happens randomly, as your ego would have you believe. Rather, all events are part of the well-orchestrated unfolding of truth upon your plane. If you were to look around, you would see that those who have suffered some sort of loss are oftentimes the ones who have learned something about life and are now carrying out their plans for perpetuating truth. There is always a reason for all that which occurs in your lifetime, and we can assure you that there is always a grand purpose to your pain. That purpose always lies within the parameters of Truth.

You, from your higher perspective, have created the Earth plane and all the dramas within it in order to learn more about who you truly are. Once you've come to the realization that you do not die––that nothing dies––you will then be able to rise above the ego state of nonsense, thereby recognizing that your earthly lives are merely a sort of play-acting in which you have chosen to take part. The belief in death is by far the greatest hurdle for mankind to overcome, and once this is accomplished, you shall be able to see clearly that as you don physicality, you are merely "stepping into character" in order to fulfill your role as your present personality in the play called earth-life. It is really that simple, dear ones; you are just in the habit of making too much of all this.

When it seems as if your prayers are not being answered, know that the universe is forever at your beck and call, and that it answers all your needs. However, you are not always consciously aware of your greater needs, your higher intentions, from your current level of consciousness. In other words, the universe must first respond to the "blueprint" your Higher-Self has laid out for you, and this is because you designed it that way. This is the only way to the ultimate goal, which is to bring yourselves and your planet to the highest level of awareness. You are merely interacting here upon this physical plane in order to become more aware of that highest state of "Godliness" within your very own being.

Dear friends, we understand the difficulty you may be having deciphering our words because of the state of confusion in which you find yourselves currently enmeshed. But our purpose it to help those who want to rise above the current state of confusion and come Home, where peace, love and Truth abound.

Now, we must point out before ending that even though you have a blueprint of sorts which you've intended to follow during your lifetime on Earth, this does not mean it is written in stone. At all times do you have free will, and you are therefore free to alter your course at any time you see fit. You need only make your intentions known and the universe will offer assistance. But in order to accomplish this, you need to accompany your requests to alter your plans with the same intensity of emotion you had when you first laid them out. What we mean by this is that while you are praying for changes in your life to occur, you must offer the intensity of emotion which comes with belief. Then the universe will successfully do your bidding. This is what Jesus meant when he said: "And all things, whatsoever ye shall ask in prayer, believing, ye shall receive." (Matthew 21:22)

Therefore, realize that all prayers are answered on some level of your being, and all that which you experience in your day to day life was mapped out by you, and for you, as a means to higher learning. All is well and the plan is perfect. Simply put your trust in the Divine hands of the universe and allow it to teach you what it may. You must remember that the universe itself is who you are, and at all times do you pull the strings, whether you are consciously aware of it or not.

Death

Imagine that in one fell swoop, you leave behind all the cumbersome beliefs of negativity and illusion, and rejoin the billions of souls freefalling through the heavens, blissfully singing and dancing in unison. As you awaken and shake the cobwebs of forgetfulness from your mind, the memory of who you really are becomes pristine, and we hear many proclaim, "How could I have ever forgotten the magical being of light and love that I am?" And our answer is always the same: Because you're *good*. You are such powerful creators that you are capable of creating illusions which seem so real that you fool even yourself, you see.

This is the closest we can come to depicting the death experience. We've got news for you, friends. Although we hate to spoil all the fun you've been having with your belief in death and the agony associated with grief, we are here to tell you once and for all, to set the record straight: Death is an illusion. Period.

The illusion of death was created for a reason, and it has served to propel many who have experienced the loss of a loved one toward questioning their true identity. *Is it no wonder that when comparing all the paths which lead Home, grief is, by far, the most trodden?* But you've milked this illusion for all it's worth, and it's now time for humanity to lay claim to the higher states of perception, of awareness, so that you may get on with the business of living, rather than dying.

Make the decision to give up all false beliefs which support anything other than eternal life, and you shall simultaneously be giving yourself permission to *live*, which was your intent in the first place. You did not come forth into this physical arena of life to tread lightly in a pond, dear souls. You came forth to ride the majestic tidal waves of earth-life adventure, and you do so by diving in, knowing full well you'll be supported by those of us (that greater aspect of yourself) remaining on this side of the veil.

We would encourage you to stand apart from your everyday beliefs for a moment and pit the belief in death against the scientific data you've gathered thus far. Your scientists have known for some time that energy is the basis of all life existing anywhere in the universe, including that of your physical self. Have you ever tried to kill energy? Have you ever seen it die? Of course not, for you know that energy doesn't die; it simply recycles itself from one form into another. Science refers to this as "The Law of the Conservation of Energy", which states that the total amount of energy present within your universe remains a constant; it never fluctuates.

Now, think about this for a moment. Physics has already proven that everything—you included—is energy. You know that energy does not go away; it merely recycles itself, taking on various forms, such as that of water and vapor. And your great scientists have shown you that the amount of energy present in your universe never fluctuates one iota.

Add these together and what do you get? Life, dear ones, eternal, exquisite, non-ending, ever-changing life. Can you see, from this perspective, the preposterousness of a notion such as death?

Begin now to rid your consciousness of all beliefs which say that death exists, and yours shall be the Kingdom right now, right here on earth. No need to wait for evolution, you know.

Where Is the Earth Headed at This Time?

The Earth is headed "due Home", and by this we mean that you will get here, one way or another. You shall eventually have your Heaven on Earth, and right now you are in the process of making this dream a reality. Each thought you think and every circumstance you encounter serves to bridge the gap between ignorance and knowledge. Our final and most important message to you is this: Lighten up, children, and enjoy your experiences here on Earth. This is not the end-all to your being-ness. You are eternal beings with an eternity in which to explore and savor all the vastness and variety of life the universe has to offer.

You need not take your earth-life experiences so seriously. Instead, begin to recognize who you truly are and your purpose for being human. Earth life reality is a game, dear peoples, and you are encouraged to wake up and see it as such. It is a play in which you have chosen to don certain characteristics to form a particular personality so that you may interact with one another on this stage of life. We would encourage you to sing and dance your way Home, and as you do so, life will take on the essence of a warm, gentle breeze that caresses your soul. This was the intended way, and it shall be your way, if only you allow it. Release the illusion of negativity and separateness, and yours shall be the Kingdom of Heaven. So be it, dear children, so be it.

CHAPTER EIGHT

Final Thoughts on the Power of Thought

"You are like children in the cockpit of a jet plane, with enormous power in your hands and not a clue about how to control it."

"It's no accident that the words 'live' and 'love' are so similar. Anything less than perfect love can only be construed as death."

The Apostles

Author's note: Nearly two years after having completed the first seven chapters of this manuscript, I was "instructed" to add an additional chapter to help clarify our role in the grand scheme of creation and hopefully to expand your awareness about the nature of life on Earth.

By now, you're probably aware that thought is a causative power. But you may not be aware of the exact function your thinking plays in the unfolding of your everyday life experiences. After reading this chapter, you'll know, without a doubt, your place in the process of creation, enabling you to step into your power with grace and with ease. Read on. The journey continues.

What's the Purpose Behind the Duality, the Contrast, of Our World?

Contrast is the basis of your entire world. It's the foundation upon which all else is built. You're aware that the physical eye sees all things in an upside-down fashion, for as an object within your field of vision falls upon the retina in the eye, it's inverted by the brain, thereby producing an upside-down image which appears to you to be right side up. This is analogous to how all things are perceived in your world. Indeed, your entire world is a mirror image of Reality. However, it's an upside-down image of which humanity is currently in the throes of turning right side up.

This is the process of evolution, and it's also the basis for the challenge of Earth life experience. The purpose behind the creation of your upside-down world can be likened to something as simple as the reason you might sit down to work a crossword puzzle; you do it for the thrill, the challenge, the stimulation of it, which helps you to better understand your innate capabilities.

Let us offer you an easy way in which to differentiate between Reality and illusion. Take everything you've ever been taught within your world of duality, all concepts that you've ever accepted as true, and mentally place them upon one side of a coin. Now, to easily understand the way things really work, simply flip the coin over––there you'll find Truth.

All things in your world of contrast are the exact opposite of the way things really are. For example, if you've always believed in the concept of death, what's on the other side of the coin? Exquisite, never-ending, always evolving, eternal life. And that, dear ones, is Reality. If you've been led by your physical senses to believe that all things are separate from and outside of yourself, what's the opposite of this concept? Oneness. The truth is that you are indeed one with all that you perceive in your life experience, and all that you perceive is within you. The world of form is simply a projection, or an out-picturing, of the inner world of Mind.

If you've always believed yourself to be powerless and incapable of necessitating your life's direction, ask yourself what is the opposite of such a limiting belief? The truth is that no one but you has the power to dictate the direction your life will take. Understand that *you* are in complete control here. *You* are the captain of your ship. The universal principle of life, the organizing mechanism which exists at the quantum level of physical reality, is at all times merely awaiting your command instructing it about how to line up and what to *become.*

The purpose of life on Earth is expansion. The basis of all life is growth. And the impetus behind growth is desire. However, desire first needs to be kindled, and it's the contrast of your world that does the kindling, you see. As you frolic within your contrasting world, experiencing things that are not pleasing to you, you're eventually catapulted into a place of desire by your intention to seek a more pleasant experience. In other words, contrast serves as the bridge between what you're currently experiencing and that which you desire to experience. The only way that expansion can occur is for an aspect of the Universal Mind (you) to reach a place of new and clear desire, thereby activating the intent to create something new and better than what had previously been available to you. Thus, you must first experience that which you don't want in order to determine what it is you do want.

And that, dear souls, is the purpose behind your contrasting world. How would you ever know that you want more closet space unless you had first experienced a lack of closet space? How would you know that peace is your desire unless you had first experienced the ravages of war? Thus contrast is a highly effective tool which enables you to construct a world to your liking.

Contrast is certainly an asset if you choose to see it as such. However, what we've noticed is that most of you tend to see contrast as something that needs to be eradicated from your life so that you may enjoy a more peaceful existence. Again, as with all perceptions in your world, this concept is the complete opposite of Truth. You've simply gotten into the habit of attempting to push against, or resist, the contrast, when all you really need to do is embrace it and love it for all that it has offered you in the form of new desire and ultimately new creations.

Once you've perused the contrast and reached a place of new desire about something, simply allow yourself to be spring-boarded into the realization of your new desire. No longer wallow in the opposing concept which brought you to your place of desire. Instead, thank the contrast, then immediately turn around and dive joyfully into the experience of your new desire without looking back. And, from your new perspective, we can assure you that it won't be long before you'll run into some new contrast which will serve to bring you to a new place of desire, once again setting into motion the repetition of the process of creation.

Dear ones, this is the standard operating procedure of life. This is the way in which you create new heavens, new worlds and new paradigms. And this process is impossible without your willingness to interact within it. Therefore, pat yourself on the back for a job well done. For Earth is indeed on the fast track to the heavenly realms, thanks to your involvement in the eternal, efficacious, contrasting unfoldment of the majestic physical universe.

Follow your heart and be guided to the truth about your inner power. See the world not as a dark and desolate state of existence. Rather, see the darkness as the springboard upon which you'll soar into the light of Truth. Bless the darkness, dear souls. Bless yourself. Bless *all* of life, and blessings shall be all you'll reap.

Exactly what is the mind's role in creation?

Let us begin by stating that there is nothing that occurs in your life experience, be it within your body or outside of it, that is not the direct result of an intention that you hold. Intention, mind and will are interchangeable terms. Any time you hold an intention about anything whatsoever, you are using the power of Mind to exert your will. Your intention immediately causes the wheels to begin churning, setting into motion the creation of that which is the object of your intention.

How powerful is your intention? Let us offer you an exercise which will prove beyond doubt the power of your own will. Place your attention upon the big toe of your right foot. Now wiggle it. What was the cause behind the movement of your toe? Nothing but pure intent. *Your* pure intent.

We want you to understand that your ability to will your big toe to move is the same ability you have in all areas of your life. It's as simple to move a mountain through the power of pure intent as it is to move your big toe. The only difference lies in your beliefs. You believe that mountains are immovable and, therefore, they are. You believe your toe is movable and, therefore, it is. Do you see how this works?

Dear ones, you have the innate authority within you to affect *all* of life by utilizing the same power that enabled you to wiggle your toe. Can you not see the power you brandish by your very own intentions? Is it not clear to you that your toe (or anything else, for that matter) is incapable of movement without the will of your mind behind it?

In order to understand your own power, you need only turn inward and direct all your attention to the thinker behind every thought and subsequent action that occurs in your daily life. We can assure you that nothing occurs in your experience without your input, for you are the wielder of intention.

Know that *you* are the sole (soul) power behind all the events and circumstances that you experience in every moment of your existence. No one but you has the authority to direct your life experience. The mind is the ultimate and only source of creation, and you were endowed with all the creative prowess of the Universal Mind that spawned you. Ponder this: The wing of a bird was designed to support the *mind's* ability to fly. The wing by itself has nothing whatever to do with flight. Thus, a bird can fly, not because it has wings, but because it has the mind, the will, to take flight.

The next time you feel you have no control over your life, or that you're being pulled in every direction other than one that is pleasing to you, refocus your thoughts and remember the power of your mind and your ability to move your big toe. You hold the key to the entire Kingdom within your very own piece of the Universal Mind. Know your power, dear ones, and use it wisely. See yourself as the *cause* of life rather than the effect.

What's the biggest mistake we make when attempting to create something in our life?

First of all, we would like to say that there are no mistakes, dear ones, merely growth. Therefore, all that you create and experience during your lifetime serves to bring you closer to the awareness of who you *really* are. In other words, regardless of the outcome of your creations, you're nonetheless serving to bridge the gap between humanity's ignorance of its true power and the heaven state of awareness.

Now to answer your question: the biggest misperception that many of you hold is the belief that you can push against something unwanted and effectively eliminate it from your life experience. But we are here to tell you that there is no such thing as exclusion. There is only *inclusion* into your experience of more of whatever it is you give your attention to (or something of a similar frequency), wanted or not.

You must understand that whatever you focus upon, whatever it is you choose to give your attention to, expands within the perceptual framework of your life experience. This includes the "bad" as well as the "good." (In Reality, there is no "good" or "bad," but we are referring to that which is perceived as either good or bad from your perspective.)

For example, let's say you've decided that you wish to experience a new job. As you sort through the contrasting data of your present job and begin piecing together the idea of a job that is more to your liking, the universe immediately begins to put it all together for you. If you would simply stay focused upon the idea of a new and better job, holding a clear image in your mind about how a new job might enhance your life, you would quickly find yourself inundated with all sorts of job opportunities from which to choose.

However, the behavioral habit that most of you display goes something like this: 1) you have the desire for change 2) you decide that the area of your life you wish to change is that of your job 3) you then spend all of your time focused upon what it is that you dislike about your current job in an attempt to push against and hopefully eliminate it from your experience by force, all the while wondering why your situation doesn't change.

Dear ones, this scenario describes what is truly the ultimate in human dilemmas, for we see you utilizing the contrast of your world to create new desires for yourself, but this is often where the chain of creation gets broken down. Once you've utilized the contrast to bring yourself to a state of desire, your only job then is to allow the contrast to "springboard" you from the old job and into the realization of a new and better job. However, you've gotten in the habit of staying within the contrast, of keeping your attention focused upon that which you don't want, which only serves to bring you more of what you don't want. Do you see how this works?

Picture yourself at a buffet-style restaurant. As you move through the buffet line beholding all the savory choices before you, you get to choose which items to put on your plate. In this situation you understand your power of choice and your free will to choose only those items that you wish to taste. However, if you were to approach the buffet in the same manner in which many of you approach life, you might find yourself demanding that legislation be passed banning the sale of all brussel sprouts for fear that they may spread and eventually crowd out the dessert section.

Sounds silly, does it not, to think that you would approach a situation so clearly full of choices in this manner? Yet this is precisely what you do when you attempt to push against or resist anything that you don't want in your life experience. The way you approach the buffet line is with an awareness that allows you to pick and choose the items you want on your plate while you ignore those items that aren't pleasing to you. Although brussel sprouts may not be something you'd choose for yourself, you nonetheless realize that they exist for the pleasure of those who do wish to add some to their plate, and you're okay with that. You know there will always be room for the items that are appetizing to you.

Now, our point is that if you would simply approach *all* of life in the same manner that you approach the buffet table, you'd be much better off. Begin to see life as the smorgasbord of choice that it truly is and choose for yourself the people, things and events that are palatable to you, and leave the rest of it alone. It's that simple. If mashed potatoes are to your liking, simply add some to your plate. If a new job is your desire, add it to your plate. If a new home with more closet space is what you're seeking, pile it on, you see. And don't worry if you choose an item that doesn't taste as good as you had anticipated. Simply return to the buffet table and choose again.

It's as easy to change your choices in life as it is to grab a clean plate. Let go of the belief that the choices you make in this (or any) moment have to remain with you for the rest of your life. Your life is comprised of an infinite number of choices during each moment of your existence. Therefore, look not to your past as gospel or to your future as being set in stone. You truly have the power of the entire universe within you at this very moment and are therefore, at all times, unlimited in your ability to choose. When things aren't going so well for you, simply choose again by deciding to focus upon something that makes your heart sing. Your "singing heart" will then summon to you all manner of good things.

Can you offer more clarification about inclusion versus exclusion?

Again, there is no such thing as exclusion. There is only inclusion into your experience of more of whatever it is you give your attention to (or something like it), wanted or not. For example, let's suppose that you've been giving your attention to a disease such as cancer. Now let's assume that your intentions regarding cancer entail keeping it as far away from you as possible. "I do not want cancer," you say, "therefore keep it away from me." With such a statement, you're attempting to push against something that you don't want, believing that you can exterminate it from your experience. However, all that you've really managed to do is invite into your experience the very thing you do not want (and more things like it).

Why is this so? Because it's impossible to give your attention to anything without simultaneously offering an invitation for it to join you in your life experience. Thus it can be said that attention and invitation are synonymous.

In other words, you cannot exclude cancer from your experience by pushing against it, for the very act of pushing against something requires that you first place your attention upon it. Therefore, it would be wise for you to get in the habit of placing your attention only upon those things that you want to experience while ignoring the rest. If health and vitality are what you wish to add to your buffet plate, then focus on health and vitality. If joy is what you're craving, then heap it on by turning your attention to something that serves to bring you joy. And if you want to experience a healthy portion of all that is good, get yourself centered in the love vibration and you'll find your life filled with more peace, joy and prosperity than you're capable of imagining. (See the section called "Define Love" for more information on this topic.)

The next time you find yourself attempting to push against something by shouting "no" at it, stop and notice this habit while holding the intention to correct it. Correction is the process of healing your perceptions. Thus the only true correction, the only true healing, is simply the readjustment of your perceptions. Ignore everything that enters your field of perception which does not serve to enhance your awareness of the reality of goodness and love, and whatever it is will dissipate from your experience as swiftly as a cloud of dust might settle back to the ground.

You have the power, dear ones, to create your life experience in any fashion you choose to do so. And your power lies in your ability to recognize and understand the rules of the game of creation. To sum it all up, the rules of the game are as follows:

1) All that exists is energetic and magnetic in nature.

2) You, as an energetic/magnetic being, are always offering a signal, a beacon, which is continually and without interruption being matched by the universe with more things, people and circumstances that match the nature of your signal (an example of like attracting like).

3) You can always tell what mode your signal is in, and therefore what you're currently attracting to yourself, by the way the inner reflection of that signal feels. This inner reflection, or signal, is called emotion. Good emotion means positive-mode signal, and bad, or unpleasant emotion, means negative-mode signal.

4) Your signal is the result of something you're thinking about which in turn is the result of something you're either observing or imagining. Your observations and imaginings always (not just sometimes) coalesce into an emotional state, thereby producing the signal that is offered to the universe to be matched with other like signals. It matters not whether your signal is the result of your observation or your imagination. You can choose how you produce a signal. In other words, if there's nothing in your field of observation that serves to enhance the way you feel, thereby producing a positive signal in the form of positive emotion, then utilize the power of your imagination to create something in your mind that does feel good. The reality is that, at every moment of your life, you're producing a signal that is summoning unto you all that which is in harmony, or in vibrational sync, with your signal. Therefore, it matters not how you arrive at the signal. All that matters is that you strive to be aware of the rules of the game of creation. As a result, you'll become a conscious and meticulous creator, in complete control of your own destiny.

5) There is no such thing as exclusion. There is only inclusion into your experience of more of whatever it is you are focused upon (or

something similar). For example, the subjects of cancer and automobile accidents may seem completely unrelated, yet they're of the same frequency. Focus upon one and you also invite the other, you see. Think inclusion, but do not fear your own power. Unwanted creations show up in your life simply to offer you the opportunity to make another choice, should you not be satisfied with what you're presently experiencing. They do not show up as punishment for being a "bad" creator. Learn to love all that which you create—the good, the bad and the ugly, as they say, for they are all *your* children, *your* creations.

Dear ones, lighten up and love yourself. Love one another. Love *all* of life, for as you do so, you will be fine-tuning your vibration and assuring yourself a clear, pure, positive, unpolluted signal to which the universe, or God, will joyfully respond in like kind. It is indeed His good pleasure to give you the Kingdom. All you have to do is ask by offering a vibration that is in harmony with it.

Define love.

The true definition of love can easily be summed up by stating that it is the combination of all positive energies. In other words, love in its entirety is peace, joy, harmony, abundance, well-being, and all else that you consider to be good, all wrapped up neatly in one pristine package. Any time you attempt to break love apart and separate it into its many aspects, you're merely compounding your confusion.

In Reality, there is only one true form of energy, which is what you call positive. However, in your world of duality, you see two forms of energy: positive and negative. In Reality, there is only the light of truth, or positive energy, and the disallowance of it, which results in your belief in negativity. For example, perhaps you've heard the analogy that you cannot enter a light-filled room and flip on a "dark switch." You can only seek a source of light and allow it to penetrate the darkened room. Therefore, to paint a clear picture, we will agree that in your world, from your perspective, you are dealing with both positive and negative energies. Now, these two seemingly separate energies are recognized by you as fear and love. Thus it can be said that fear is the combination of all that which you believe to be of a negative nature, such as anger, hatred, jealousy, greed, poverty, and so forth. In Reality, there is no such thing as hatred, there is only fear. There is no such thing as greed, for greed is also an aspect of fear. Do you see how this works? All that which you consider to be good, of God, is, indeed, love. And all that which you consider to be not so good, or lacking in the awareness of God (the light of truth), is, indeed, fear.

Imagine a golden-white ball of light, similar to the sun. Now, picture in your mind's eye what happens as you shine that golden-white light through a prism, such as water. What do you get? A rainbow, of course. A rainbow is a visual display of the various colors that are inherent within the nature of the white light itself, but which are normally undetectable to the naked eye.

Now imagine that the sun represents the energy of love and that the rainbow is analogous to positive emotion. In your attempts to separate the inherently conjoined aspects of love, you have simply "prismed" the energy of it and created what appear to be separated attributes, such as peace, joy and so forth in the same way that you perceive red, orange, yellow, green, blue, indigo and violet in a rainbow. In your world of duality, of polarity, of contrast, you have taken all that is divine—which includes all aspects of darkness and light—and have fragmented it so that everything appears to be separate. But we are here to remind you that all is, indeed, not separate. All that exists is a portion, a hologram, if you will, of the whole in its entirety. Unity is the only Truth. As you look about and detect the aspects of your world that you consider to be good, realize that all goodness is, in Reality, love. The love vibration comprises the entire gamut of peace, joy, abundance, health, unity and harmony within its very nature. Therefore, do not look to peace and joy as separate attributes. Instead, see love as the entire package of all that is necessary to seek in order for peace and joy to be your experience. Do you see how this works? In other words, love is all there is in Reality. And the love frequency encompasses all that you deem to be good. Center yourself in the vibration of love and yours shall truly be the entire Kingdom of Heaven.

Before ending, we would also like to point out the healing power of love. Love heals because it is *always* the dominant vibration. To be in love means to be in vibrational sync with peace, joy, abundance, good will, and all manner of good things. And the healing power of love results from one who consciously and deliberately vibrates within the frequency of love, thereby pulling everyone else into the same frequency. This, dear souls, is the greatest of all gifts, to be able to dominate the world with your love and to give the gift of a higher frequency to one who may be in need of it. Allow the love that is buried within you to shine forth unto the world and you shall indeed be fulfilling your purpose as a human being on planet Earth. And nevermore shall you dream of a hellish world that doesn't exist in Reality.

What Does It Mean to "Turn the Other Cheek"?

Do you know what it means to ignore something? To ignore something does not mean to run across a subject or an object you disapprove of and then spend your time and energy rationalizing why it is that you don't approve of it. Nor does it mean that you share with the world why it is that this thing of which you disapprove should also be unworthy of anyone's attention in an attempt to force your views upon someone else. To ignore simply means to turn the other cheek. It does not entail pushing against the things you don't want or don't agree with in a misguided attempt to eliminate them from your life. Get in the habit of immediately placing your attention upon something that is pleasing to you whenever you bump into something that is not pleasing. It's that simple.

Whatever you give your attention to expands or increases in your life. Should you encounter a person, place, thing or circumstance that is not up to par with your idea of perfection, turning the other cheek is an act of discernment. Spending time pondering the situation and keeping your attention focused upon why it is that the object of your attention should not be worthy of your time is an act of judgment. Do you see the difference? Wanted or not, as you hold your attention upon something, you're literally inviting it (and more things like it) into your experience. Is something that is not pleasing to you really worth the repercussions you'll surely reap by giving your attention to it? Think about it. You've heard it said that to offer judgment about something (or someone) hurts only the one doing the judging, and this is why. As you expend your precious energy in any direction whatsoever, you're literally trading or bartering your energy for the manifestation of an experience that matches the object (or subject) of your attention. See the creative force of your attention as a medium of exchange and guard the manner in which you spend it very carefully, for you will be purchasing access to the object of your attention as surely as if you had exchanged money for the purchase of an item.

As you retrain your mind to remove its focus from something you don't want and immediately place it upon something you do want, you are being a deliberate, conscious, intentional creator. And this, dear ones, is the wisdom of a master. Each of you holds within yourself this master potential. All you have to do to let your true light shine is learn to wield your creative powers wisely by holding as the object of your attention *only* that which is pleasing to you. Learn to be as picky about the things you give your attention to as you are about the foods you put in your mouth, and your world, your life experience, will dramatically change for the better.

But don't take our word for it. Prove to yourself the power you wield with the sword of intention. See if being finicky about what you give your attention to doesn't result in profound changes in your life. Stop giving away your power by letting your attention be pulled in a myriad of directions. Instead, seize the reins, move into the driver's seat, and deliberately, intentionally, consciously command the direction of your thoughts, for this, dear souls, is precisely what you've come to this planet to do. *You* are the only true power here.

ABOUT THE AUTHOR

K.C. Kymball is a no-nonsense, show-me-the-facts, scientifically-oriented person who believed the idea of channeling information from otherworldly beings was pure lunacy. Until it happened to her.

During her experience with grief after the unexpected death of her beloved sister, she began searching for the meaning of life. Her search led to the discovery of an innate ability to receive profound, loving messages from unconventional sources. The wisdom she receives has served as a catalyst in helping many people understand their true nature and the astonishing degree of personal power concealed within each and every individual.

K.C. resides in Nashville, TN and is currently working on a book and educational program designed to radically transform our world's outdated perceptions of grief, death, heartache and loss. For more information, feel free to contact the author at KC.Kymball@mail.com or by visiting http://www.KCKymball.com.

Have you ever wondered why you were born? Does your life have a sense of purpose? Is there a rationale behind all the beauty and magnificence of our world, behind the chaos and strife? What does it all mean? Where are we headed and from where have we come? These are the toughest of the tough questions and this book provides comprehensive, relatable, common-sense answers. Read it now and allow your confusion to dissipate and your confidence, in yourself and others, to soar.

"If I could read only one book, this would be it. A must for every spiritual seekers library."
–– Patricia Mischell, author of *Beyond Positive Thinking*

"If you're searching for a path to discovering a profound level of inner peace and wisdom, this book points the way."
— Stacey Johnson, owner, 2XL Coaching

"This book will show you how to harness the power of your mind and steer your life in a conscious, meaningful direction."
— Sheri Evans, Yoga Instructor, Beverly Hills, California

Printed in the United States
By Bookmasters